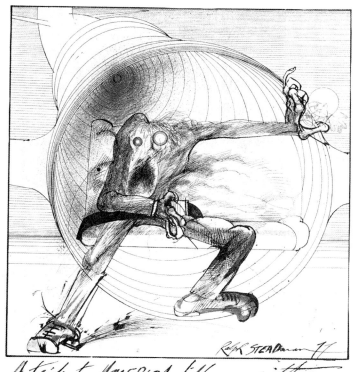

A trip to AMERICA fills me with
anticipation

HARRAP
London

SCAR STRANGLED BANGER

Ralph STEADman

To John Lambe.
And to all those who say they
don't like the sound of America and
have never been there – this book
I absently dedicate . . .

Contents

First published in Great Britain 1987
by HARRAP Limited
19-23 Ludgate Hill, London EC4M 7PD

© Ralph Steadman 1987

ISBN 0 245 54420 8

Designed by Langley Iddins
Printed and bound in Italy
by arrangement with Graphicom, Vicenza

THERE SOMEWHERE

'We have room for but one language here, and that is the English Language, for we intend to see that the crucible turns our people out as AMERICANS.'

Teddy Roosevelt

Definition of a BAN

BANGER is a word used for the much-loved English sausage, but what that has to do with your constitution, God on

BANGER is a word used to describe a kind of automobile, or an automobile in a certain condition, which only got into its present state due to a life filled with eventful and uncertain driving techniques. These would have been imposed upon it by an unthinking, insensitive, indifferent and countless succession of drivers, whose only reason for paying any attention whatsoever to the car is that it gets them from A to B, sometimes. They would only be addressing themselves to it when it either refuses to go or they wish to climb inside it in order to give it another go. A healthy attitude towards a piece of utility junk.

When it doesn't go, it is kicked, rocked, cursed, wept over bitterly, even loved, and occasionally beaten ceremoniously with anything heavy or close to hand, like a big spanner or a car repair manual. It will have seized up, boiled up, cracked up, been driven out of hell, crushed, kicked, repainted, driven over trenches, thrown over cliffs and left to rot on the hard shoulders of freeways. When you finally curse the very day you ever set eyes on it and decide to sell it, you cannot find words grand enough to describe how reliable it is. How you will be sorry to see it go and how you will miss it like an old friend – and, if the new owner gets half the pleasure out of it that you have had, he's going to have a helluva good time with it.

I use the word BANGER in the context of this book as a euphemism, not for your flag, but for your constitution. If you think back over the years, whilst you have loved it, you have also abused it, and yet it still works. You have cursed it, kicked it, twisted it to mean what you want it to mean, but ultimately it got you where you want to be. With your liberties unimpaired and your rights still clearly defined, no matter how far you have strayed from some earlier course. It is still working as Thomas Jefferson intended it to work, when he said don't just talk about your rights, but commit them to paper, so that they may be referred to at all times and be understood by all. That was by far the greatest development in the history of democracy since the Greeks invented it.

ows, and I wouldn't be so cute as to try and suggest a connection. But you now have a whole new word to slang around.

INTRODUCTION

I think it is fair to say, or at least to suggest, speaking as a clear rounded Welshman who rather thinks about these things off and on, without prejudice, or at least without qualms – not enough to keep me awake at nights anyway, over and above my normal individual's share, that is – and maintaining objectivity, in the face of opposition, and given that this is not a perfect world, or even a world fit for human habitation, let alone animals who deserve our consideration, and getting to the point, but before I do, because there is always time, and people should exercise patience above all things, save compassion, easing their point forward in an atmosphere of brotherly anticipation and soothing reflection, a moment of pause, before a possible misunderstanding, and who for? you may say, but 'who for?' is at the root of your compassion, if you have any, if you can afford any, well to even like people to think you have, that in itself is a sign – but only a sign, not a confirmation, a certainty, a dead certainty, something real, to depend upon, that may suggest, well not suggest, but pass over,

something inside you, deep, something deeper, inside you, a heart maybe, not a heart, perhaps a regulated impulse output module, something like that, to accept what I think it is fair to say about you, the Americans as a nation, that, and this is where it becomes very difficult, only inasmuch as you may simply object on principle to the slightest hint of criticism, albeit if firmly proffered with a total absence of malice and with the best of intentions, skipping lightly over the groundswell, whilst choosing my words very, very carefully, so carefully, in fact, that there are hardly any I can use without someone, always someone, taking unreasonable exception to what after all is a gesture of friendship, a nudge in the ribs, with a wink, of course, that, and this is where we get into deep water, and sometimes I wish I had never started this, or that, but once started, you know how it is, you have to follow through to the bitter end, get it out, leave nothing smouldering only to fester, thoughts, like split atoms, a fact of life, practically in the throes of gouging out of my self, and by the way, I know quite a few, quite a lot, of

Americans, good Americans, and many of persuasions that cannot be categorised, the nearly weird and the weird, the drivers and the losers, the nearly rich and the badly scarred, friends, no enemies, each understands the other, marks out an area, a space to be in, for the others, they will understand, but only just, they will know I mean well, well enough to get to the point without injury, so much so that I think it is fair to say that, and time to say that, Americans are a bunch of rejects, whoops! a dying breed, well, hardly a breed. Breeding requires certain genetic structures, premeditated intentions and social instructions of a rarified nature. That is, good breeding. Animals breed, involuntarily, so we are talking about breeding as a specific, a sustained aspiration, a pinnacle of human excellence, a plateau of limited space, for a select few, not millions. Without prejudice – we are up here, you are down there.

It's not your money. Your money won't help. So, a dying breed, Americans. Maybe you are already dead. A dead breed, yes, mutating your dead souls for world domination. A dying breed suggests no future, but you, the dead, you have nothing to fear. Communism, weirder immigrants, annexation, ethnic cultures, none of it. You have it all, all of you, some of you so powerful. So big. A nation in its youthful death. Glowing and growing. Growing pains. Adolescent death. Heartache and growing. A pulsing tribal pride. A nation of fugitives – fugitives from the earthiness of the rest of us. We are living with our mistakes, turning them into fertiliser, but you are clean, clear of the dust and muck, starting life on a new veneer. A huddled mass on a new veneer, dismembered and scared, but clear and with reason to hope. Unity and difference. Vested interest and diverse unreason. A diabolic purpose, a forging of destiny. The veneer thickens . . .

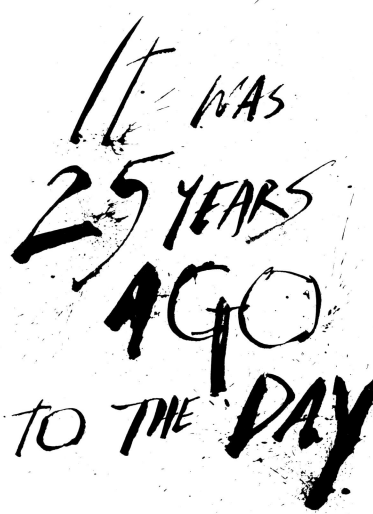

Twenty-five years ago I burned with a passion to change the world. I also imagined that people were reasonable and would change with it. I thought that there were good people, which included me, and I knew that there were bad people who would change when they saw the error of their ways.

I thought that in my lifetime we would see peace, harmony, love, prosperity for all, a gentle tolerance of the diversity of opinion and a generosity of spirit enough for all to flourish.

Twenty-five years ago I thought that people believed in fair play and, given an explanation, would make allowances for another's mis-demeanours. I was sure that we were through the bad bit and human suffering would be a thing of the past. I was sure that we would build upon what we had learned, and I was certain that, with time, old sores would heal, old grudges would die and old policies would be revised and changed to accommodate our new enlightenment.

What I thought would happen, God only knows, but twenty-five years later I still feel the same.

Only my drawings tell you what I was doing; and, as I finish this last sentence, the natural light is dying and I am going to have to turn on the desk lamp and spoil everything.

The Quality of Life

Quality of life in America conjures up certain
connotations in my bruised mind.

Quality of life conjures up a kind of lifestyle that
includes buckwheat and rye bread, freshly-
squeezed oranges, tennis courts, squash players,
hunting, fishing, and spotting brown bears.

Quality of life is a camping site in the
Appalachian foothills, two kids and your own
mobile home. This situation may also include eggs
any style, but mainly 'up', Club sandwiches,
roller skating, and lettuce with everything including a mountain range of dressings from Blue cheese
to something Americans call 'French' dressing –
but which is in fact Italian.

To enjoy this Quality of life you need to be
young, even though you are not, well-tanned all
over, preferably well-off and having a nice day.

The Quality of life is a clean mind and a healthy body. The pleasant nature of the disciples of this state of mind declares a wholesome emptiness, an offensively outgoing bonhomie, a disarming lack of direction, and a heartfelt conviction that, even though you may have just pissed on their sneakers, life is 'just great'. No problems darken the brow above the gentle sunburned shadows around their eyes which look out upon the world and you, with the equanimity of reptiles spread-eagled on a hot rock.

The Quality of life includes jogging, back-slapping, drive-in banks, perfume shops on Rodeo Drive, Beverly Hills and silicone transplants. The very young are given to believe that the Quality of life is written in neon lights and July 4th celebrations, making deals in Jacuzzis and Sunday newspapers four inches thick. The Quality of life is keeping the very old alive until the eyes in their sockets just barely stay in place, or hang in there like ping pong balls in jars of cold cream. The Quality of life is an alternative lifestyle, bussing blacks and Saturday Night Specials, All-Nite Liquor stores, aerobic workouts and Frank Sinatra. It is, and always will be, the limitless opportunities that such a monstrous country offers to anyone, and not everyone, to get in there and mine it for themselves in any field from nuclear physics to Cabbage-Patch dolls. No discretion is necessary or even called for. Its very brashness produces the quintessential quality of all their lives – one helluva pile of money.

Overheard Ageing southern lady to helpless wino on sidewalk on East 36th between 3rd and 4th (approximately).

'Why don't you get up and get a jarb? You ought to be ashamed of yo'selv. Aincha got no pride? A man ought to have pride in himself. Come on now. You ought to get up and get a jarb. You ain't a pretty sight, lyin' thar. You get up now. You get up and go clean up. You oughta have pride. People ain't got no respect if they see ya down thar. You ain't got no respect, ya hear. Get a jarb. A man oughta have a jarb. You know what arm saying. Let go that hydrant. Stand up. Take a pride in ya'self.'

'Oh leave me alone, lady.'

'That's no way to talk. Get up now and get along. Find a jarb.'

'Please, lady. Please leave me alone.'

'Now you look hear. I seen worse than you get up and get a jarb. Ya hav'ta make the first move ya'self. Now listen to what I say and get to ya feet.'

'I can't get to my feet. Please lady, please leave me alone. Please.'

'You sick or something? If ya sick I'll call an ambulance. If ya not sick then take a pride and get up.'

'Oh no, please lady, please leave me. You ain't helpin'. You just making things woise. I ain't goin' no place, I'm staying here.'

'You ain't a man. You's a bum and I ain't said that to no one before. You take a pride. You get up and get a jarb.'

'Lady, please. Just go. I'll get up. Just go. Please. Please. Leave me alone.'

'I wanna see you get up.'

'No, *I* don't wanna see me get up. Later, but not now. Just leave me.'

'You take a pride. You get up and you go find a jarb. A man oughta have a jarb. D'ya hear? You get up now. Come on. You get up, you just gotta . . .'

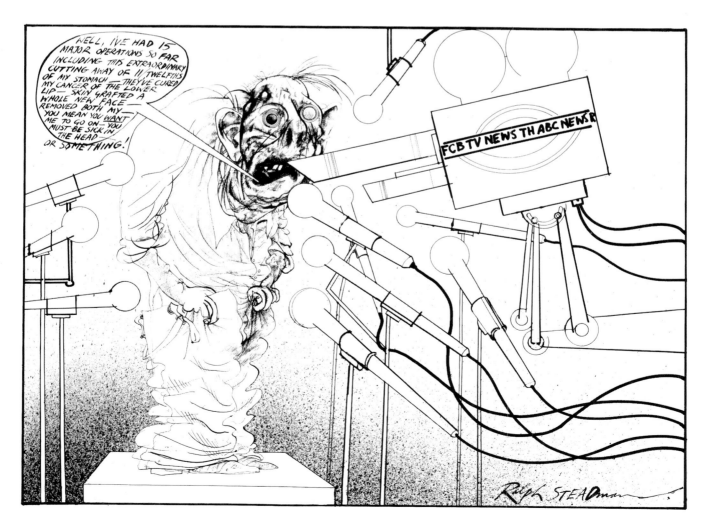

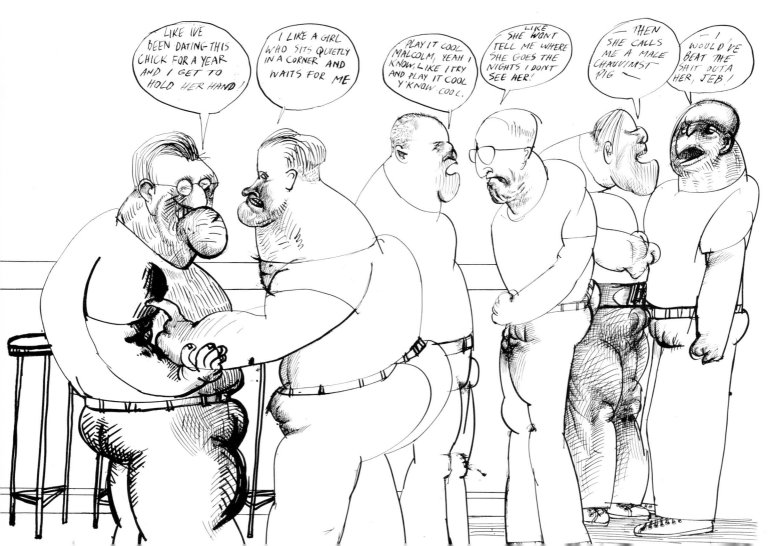

—NOT a picture of a man being sick—but a picture of a man breathing in—deeply.

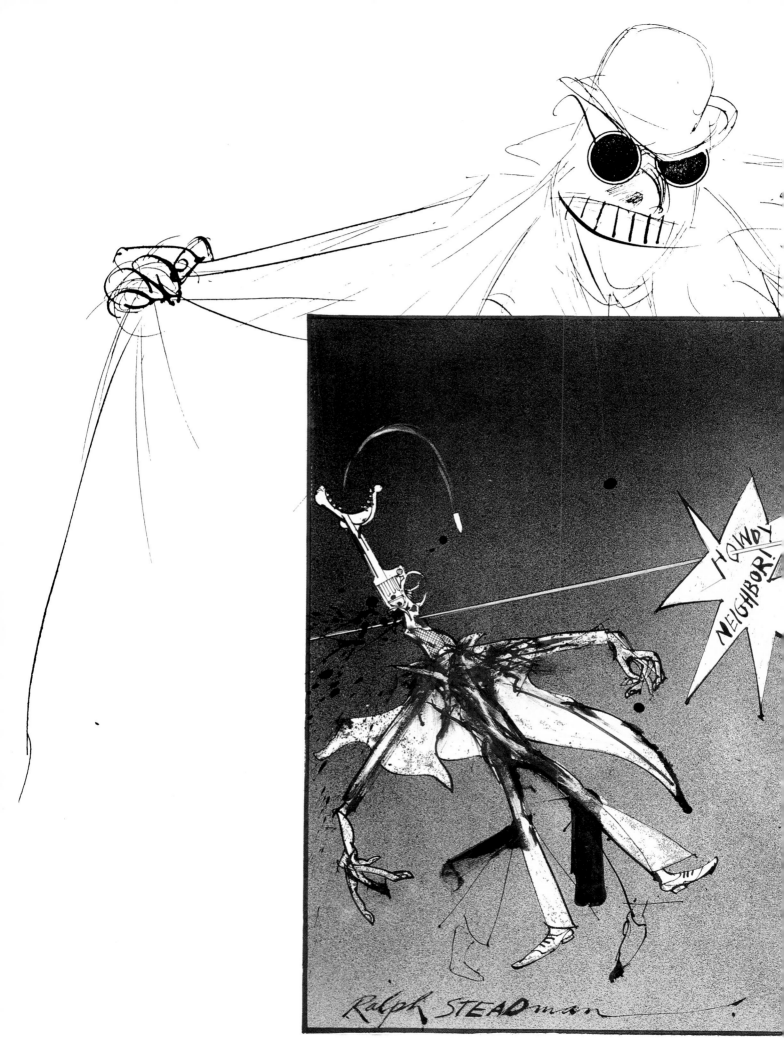

January 3, 1984
Frazier Park Office, Interstate 5, Freeway to
Bakersfield and Sacramento.

7 am. The morning was an absolute delight to
wake up to – bright and clear as a crystal vase.
There was a pleasant toytown atmosphere about the
small town of Frazier Park – a settlement toytown
with quaint home-made wooden constructions.
Clean atmosphere as we walked to the local rough-
and-ready coffee-shop to have breakfast at the
counter, shoulder-to-shoulder with burly, bluff
backwoodsmen eating honey-coated pancakes,
hash browns and two eggs over, swilling coffee and
telling crude stories of life in the old country.

Ralph STEADman 84
Frazier Park
BREAKFAST SHOP.

ENERGY CRISIS!

LANTIC CARS IN

New York experienced a violent
Fish Storm of such a perplexing
nature in the early 80's, that
New Yorkers preferred to walk about
as though everything was normal,
rather than admit that they
had a fish on their head.

IF
YOU'VE
GOT
IT
FLAUNT
IT..

BUREAU OF IDENTIFICATION
DEPARTMENT OF POLICE, CITY OF LOS ANGELES.

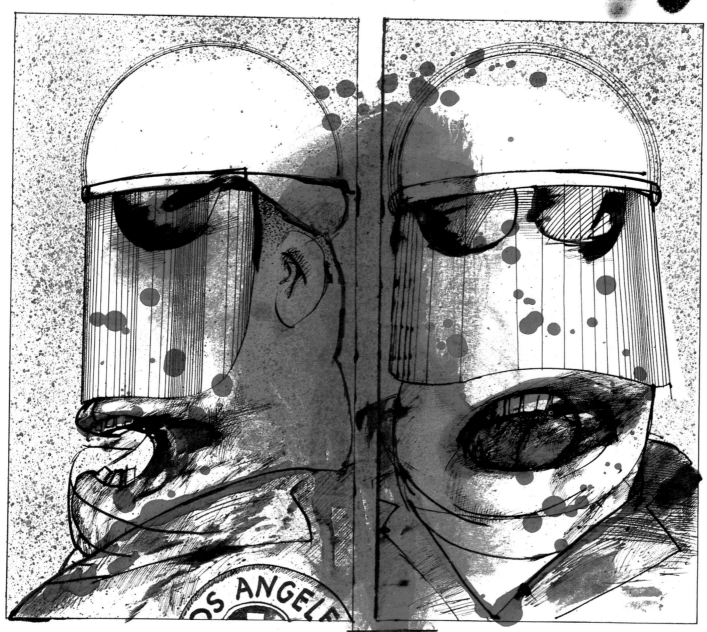

DESCRIPTIVE

San Quentin

NAME *Abe Citizen*.
Alias *Officer Citizen* (*alias Ralph STEADman* :)
County *Los Angeles*
Crime *Pig*

Reg. No. *22936*

Sentence *25* YRS.

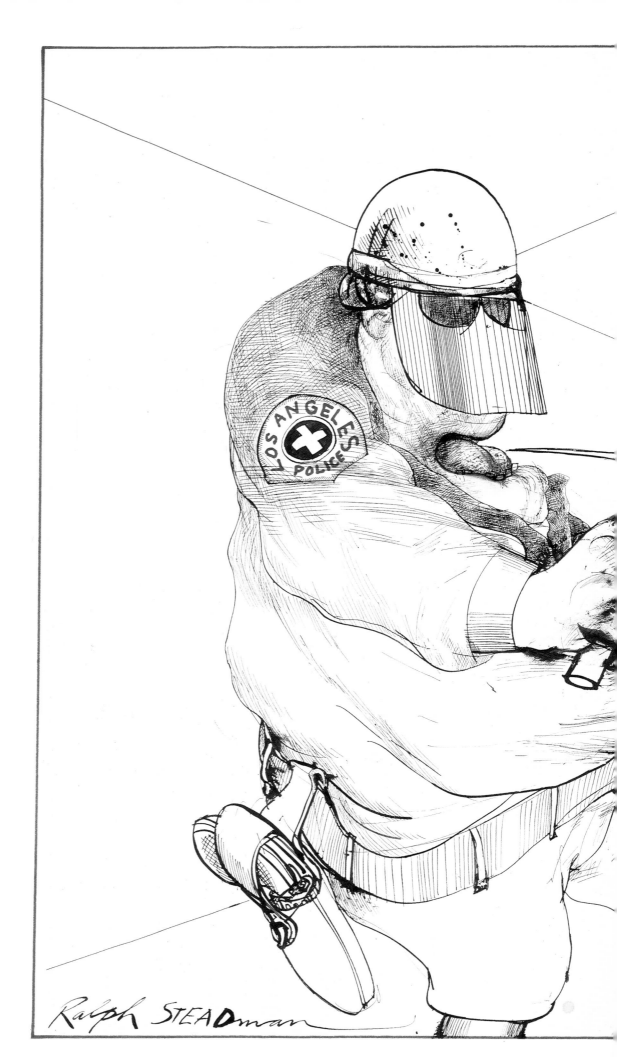

Ralph STEADman

RICHARD NIXON

—A SHORT APPRECIATION

Without a shadow of doubt, Richard Milhous Nixon was a satirist's dream. Someone to really get your teeth into. As a subject for drawing he has no equal. Those dark jowls. The eyes displaying a volatile and hazardous nature. The hangdog look of a creature made for the cut and thrust of dirty infighting. The look of a man, guilty from the cradle, rounding his shoulders into a curse. The sweep of his nose was the last thing I thought about. I only thought of the darker things. I thought of an inner turmoil spilling over the walls of a bastion of doubt. I thought of polluted mill-streams falling over cliffs and piercing the darkness of a bottomless pit. I thought of Dante and the damned.

I thought of Dante's second circle – the commencement of Hell. Carnal sinners being driven incessantly by fierce winds in total darkness. Eternal storms of heavy hail, foul water and snow. Dark water, gushing out of clefts, the prodigal and the avaricious fighting a constant battle of turmoil inside their own minds, inside *his* mind.

I thought of the souls of the wrathful and the gloomy struggling in the mud of a freshly-drained village pond. When I thought of Richard Milhous Nixon, I saw the contours of nameless objects of a troubled past smoothly covered with a fine black layer of slimy mud slowly emerging as the pool is emptied. I thought of wild chasms and shattered rocks surrounding the entrance to a downward path, to a river of blood, to the tormented souls who stand upright in its stream, up to their throats or up to their eyebrows, according to their guilt.

I thought of his piety and his pleading ways and yet I could never believe him. That was his purity. There were no half measures. His intentions were clear. He would go all the way and use his whimpering guile when things got rough.

I thought of him down among the dead men,

making bargains, scheming his next ten moves and pleading for mercy when the goods he had promised arrived, near to putrefaction. I thought of him blending with the shadows of his victims. And I saw his heart swell with rage and hold itself in check at the eleventh hour, like a corpse waiting for the verdict – was it Heaven or Hell? I saw the contrition melt the features of his face, and the wounded eyes damn his nation to an eternity of remorse. I saw him try to die on our living-room floors, milking our forgiveness, robbing us of our pity and the satisfaction of calling him Judas. Great stuff!

A satirist's dream. He has left me with a vision, and there aren't many who can do that. It's a pity he is not running again for office. We need people like Richard Milhous Nixon.

Miami Beach. 23.8.72 RSP: Mr Richard Milhous Nixon listens intently to a report by Dr Henry Kissinger, National Security Adviser, on his return from secret talks in Paris and Saigon with North Vietnamese. Before Mr Nixon gave his acceptance speech at a rally given in his honour at Miami Beach on 23.8.72, Mr Spiro Agnew stands by, waiting his instructions. (Reuter Steadman Press News. 2736096 - RSPN) 23.8.72

Little is known of this picture except that Mr Nixon (centre) suffered from a power complex, a hatred of humanity, near impotence and finally, premature senility which resembles Parkinson's Disease. Experts disagree as to whether his complex was a result of an early stage of Parkinson's Disease or an advanced stage of neuro-syphilis caught during his student days which has hallucinatory effects on the victim, giving him a sense of grandeur. The second possibility has been ruled out on the grounds that, at the time Mr Nixon was a student, it would have been socially impossible for him to contact such a disease, except, perhaps, from a lavatory seat. He died senile in an anti-environment bunker near Camp David seated before a sun-ray lamp, in a deck chair, wearing only a pair of jackboots.

Miami was subsequently reclaimed in 1982 and became an alligator swamp and tourist attraction.

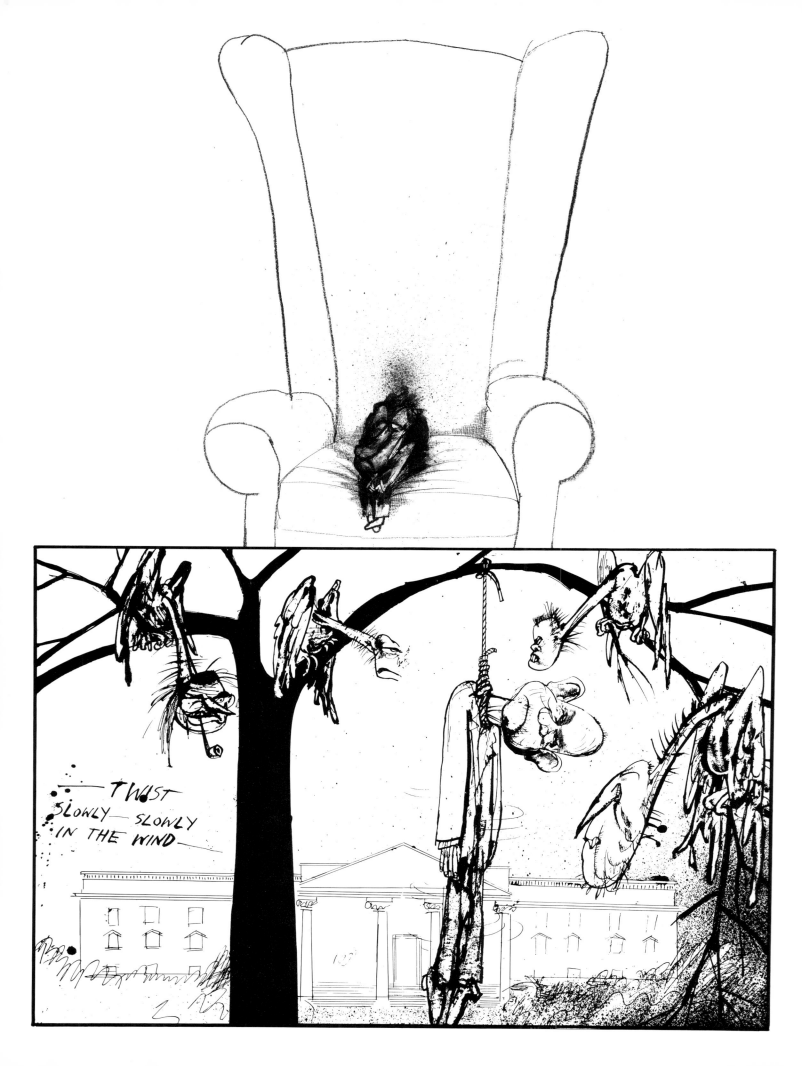

WATERGATE
WATERGATE

During the 1976 Republican Convention in Kansas City I was on an assignment for *Rolling Stone* magazine with John Dean, Nixon's ex-lawyer and adviser. I remember it well. After an initial, apprehensive meeting when we discussed the mechanics of faulty typewriters, we became very friendly, in spite of the fact that he had been a target of political satire, including my own. It turned out he knew more about typewriters than me.

During many chats, then and on subsequent meetings, he mentioned one particular situation which I think is of interest as one of the dilemmas of the young men of Watergate. Part of the dilemma was that John happens to have a photo-graphic memory for dates, times, everything. Who said what to whom, where and when, even what they were wearing at the time. And even, who lunched with whom and what they had for hors

d'oeuvres. The week before he was due to testify at the Watergate hearing and tell what he knew, he was asked by Nixon, in the company of Haldeman, Erlichman and other aides, at Camp David, whether he would be able to bend the details a little to put things in a better light for those involved. Often, on previous occasions, they had asked him, "John, what happened on such-and-such a date?" He would think for a while and be able to give them a pretty accurate answer, who said what and to whom on those specific dates. An extraordinary kind of talent. However, he found this particular request very difficult. Whilst he was an extremely ambitious man, he was, and is, as basically honest as the rest of us and it was something he could not bring himself to do. Maybe if he could have done, he would have done, for his loyalties must still have been directed towards those who had employed him. His crowd, as they still were.

During the weekend following this request and before he was due to testify, he felt physically threatened and kept himself as visible as possible, staying out of trouble until the authorities conducting the Watergate hearing had him once more under their protection.

It was a question of loyalties, but more important at that moment, a question of survival. If you have a photographic memory and you are asked to lie, you are going to get yourself into very deep water. It's not like the average mind, remembering things vaguely. A photographic mind remembers things exactly.

The young men of Watergate were all ambitious and it was that ambition, as John Dean said, that made them blind. Blind to the fact that no matter

An Historical Survey of the WATERGATE AFFAIR

MARCH '71: NIGHT FALLS. OPERATION 'SLEEP' IS INAUGURATED. (SLIMY-ENTERPRISE-TO-RE·ELECT-THE·PRES.)
PLANS ARE MADE BY A BAND OF DEDICATED FORTUNE-HUNTERS WHO FIRMLY BELIEVE THAT IF VAST
QUANTITIES OF MONEY KEEP POURING IN, IT MUST BE RIGHT.
PRESIDENT NIXON IS ASLEEP AT THIS TIME.....

MAY '71 Nixon enjoys gentle support. Muskie moves ahead of front-runner Democrats. Nixon sleeps. . . .

SUMMER '71 Pentagon Papers published in N.Y. Times. Nixon woken for split-second by trusted aide John Ehrlichman (former Seven-Up, Sani-Flush salesman) Nixon has coughing fit and relapse. . . .

JANUARY '72 Muskie ahead of Nixon in Harris Polls survey. Shadowy figures work feverishly through the long night to check the rot. FBI Chief Hoover dies carrying his secrets to the grave. . . . (Wait a minute—no he doesn't!)

MARCH '73 Nixon disturbed from sleep by grumbling murmurs of White House cleaner Martha Mitchell. Thinks it's time to say 'Howdy Folks' to the nation on TV.

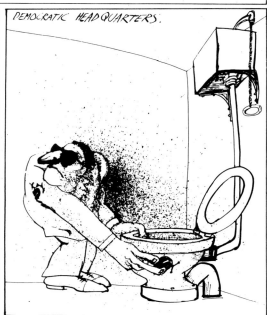

FEB-MARCH '72 Muskie stomped at New Hampshire. Democrats get nervous as new man McGovern moves ahead. Hunter Thompson gets noticed. MAY '72. Democratic headquarters at WATERGATE hotel bugged. Conventions, ballyhoo, landslide for Nixon, etc. . . . .

APRIL '73 Nixon can't sleep. Complains of domestic upsets. Says 'Howdy Folks' on TV. Consults Doctor, Sam Ervin. . . . .

WHITE HOUSE PLAYPEN

Well, that's the theory anyway . . . All the good guys go to law school.

I don't know how you legislate for honesty and decency: General Walker. John Dean suggested that the CIA did some improper things that even high officials didn't know about.

Encapsulated reason surrounded all those young men.

who was giving the orders, sooner or later somebody has to answer for them, and it's usually those in the front line.

Erlichman: He leaves no more blood on the floor than he has to.

Everyone was avoiding perjury in an attempt to reduce their sentence. Get the Hunch-back of San Clemente. Get him in his Eagle's Nest.

The left hand only knew what the right hand was doing, not what it was thinking.

Let him hang there – let him twist slowly, slowly in the wind: Haldeman about Patrick Gray about to be indicted.

I trusted and I believed and I love this country of ours: Gray, as he hung there, slowly twisting.

During the hearings Nixon declared that he was giving $3,000,000 to fight crime in the next three years.

Each one of 'em is telling a portion of the truth: Weicker (one of the Watergate Investigation Committee).

I only had a sign-off on the end product: Haldeman. Nixon aide.

Some of the papers in the safe were very politically sensitive. So far we've not answers, we've had speeches: Mr. Dash. W. Committee.

I don't quarrel with your argument, I quarrel with your paraphrasing: Erlichman.
Nixon aide under cross examination.

There is a kind of evil that has become OK.

The term 'evil', sir, is relative. I don't quite recall, sir . . . no one wants to perjure themselves.

Heard in a taxi: It's like finding out your wife's running around with someone else, and you don't want to know about it.

I'm beginning to doubt my own lies.

Government run by fifty people and the rest is show.

If we were in Germany in the old days, you'd be a lampshade and I'd be smiling: J. Gordon Liddy.

Irangate. Pearlygate. Same play. Different cast.

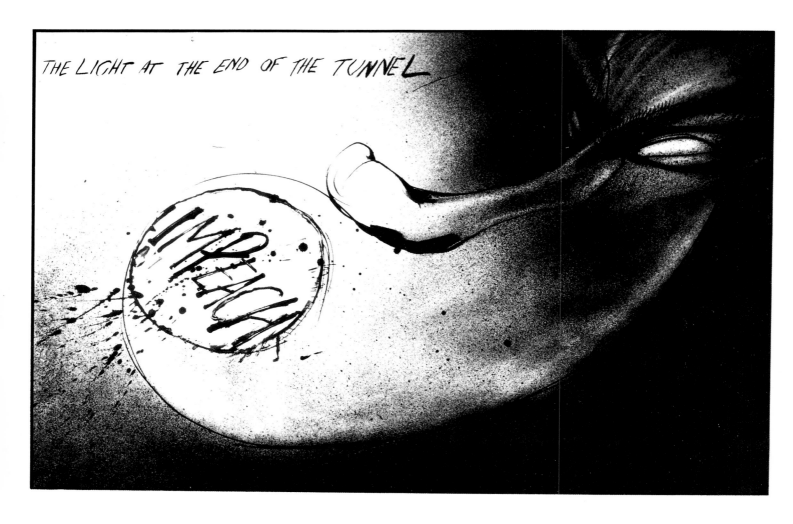

Texas has achieved the distinction of being the largest area of flat unpleasantness in the world. It is the yardstick again

hich to measure ugliness

If you are not big in Texas you are insignificant and if you are insignificant in Texas you are dead. Texans are so big that even their cockroaches cause road accidents. The only place you can walk in Texas is in the trunk of your car. If you have something small in Texas you keep it in a private place. If you haven't got a private place then you stick it up your ass. And talking of asses, Texans have the biggest asses anywhere. Bigger even than the Sumo wrestlers of Japan. In fact, bigger than a Republican Elephant's ass. Their asses are so big you sidestep half a block to pass them by. Their oil wells are so deep that they have to lease land rights from the Australian government before they drill. Their trash cans have 35 floors, high-speed lifts, and air conditioning. A library is somewhere you go if you want to live alone. If you go into a supermarket, take a cab to the checkout. Texans have more crime, more drugs, bigger rackets, and more religion than an African missionary. They have no morals, no heart, and they think that being kind is suggesting a stranger gets the hell out before they call the cops. In fact, they are so Christian, they would crucify you sooner than look at you.

And if you try wearing one of their stetsons, make sure you are a qualified hang-glider.

Hallelujah! and praise the Lawd!!

Heat, by God! The heat. Chunks of it pressing in on every part of your body. Clammy, bored people wandering about the baggage claim. Policewoman with bulging pants stands checking baggage of departing passengers. Everything has a temporary feeling – jerry-built. Frayed at the edges.

Manners change. Some folks take care to be polite but some just couldn't care less. We are staying in a reasonably pleasant, hacienda-style motel. The service is curt and to the point. Who's paying the bill? – Straight Arrow – Straight what? – Straight . . . Oh, never mind, if you'd care to call them – That won't be necessary, sir. Do you have a credit card? – No! Blank – Well, if you wish to use the bar you'll need this Guest Card. Don't lose it . . . sir! The bar is dark – the Cuatro Club. Noisy crowd of crazies sitting around a table full of empty Bud beer cans. The room is sparse but there it is – life going on. Here – out there – everywhere people sit in rooms miles from everyone, living their lives like no one else existed. If one could see all these diverse scenes simultaneously – impossible to do – but the world must be positively buzzing with movement.

Dallas is flat and shabby on the outskirts. New buildings have heat-reflecting mirror glass, mainly in gold. The freeways into the city abound with cheap eat-in places which usually stay in business about twelve months, then change hands.

Dallas has gone. It disappeared on November 22, 1963.

Nowadays it's a thriving tourist town with a live waxwork museum and the Kennedy Memorial show – nothing else at all. Except new blocks of high-rise mirror glass and a Hilton on downtown Commerce Street.

Our visit happened to coincide with the colourful, jazzy 74th Black Elk Convention held at the Hilton. A lobby full of fat, contented Duke Ellingtons, mamas, comely stetson-hatted black dollies all plump in the right parts, grandmas, grandpas – wizened, lined little deep southern faces straight off the front porches of Alabamie! Big black businessmen showing how they've made it, white-style, in their white, diamond-studded fezzes dangling huge gold tassels over their flash off-the-peg gear.

This philanthropic event, run purely on a non-profit-making basis, was filling up the Dallas Hilton to show off the Elk's achievements and themselves, and to raise money to help more deprived kids (black and white) get an education – and religion. Although the Black Panthers would also like deprived kids to have an education, their philosophies on how to achieve that aim are sorely different.

But the strong, English, middle-class streak in me applauded the almost childlike gaiety, look what we've done, ain't everybody friendly, sort of feeling that shone from their gorgeous black faces. I even felt vaguely comfortable and safe among them. Comfortable and safe is their way and that's how they like to make it. And so what, I think their zest outshone the undertones political and social, and that was nice, even though it was a convention – or a show of strength.

Beginning to feel heavy and fat. I now weigh two hundred pounds holding a pizza in each hand.

main St. couple.

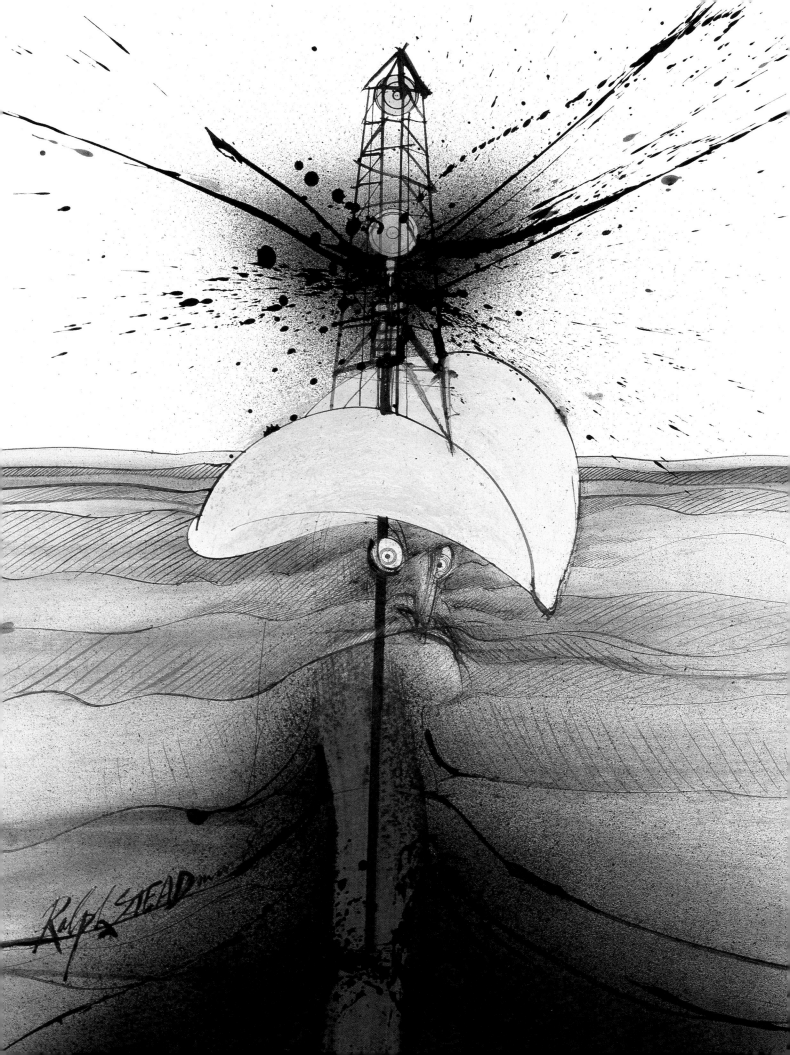

ELKS GRAND LODGE CONVENTION
DALLAS HILTON AUG.'73
BAR
GRAN
UNEXALTE
BUTT
PICKER
UPPER

We were driven around the Rich White Ghetto, having been warned beforehand that it was dangerous to walk.
As we drove I espied what appeared to be a dangerous lunatic.

Our driver Elizabeth (a lovely southern Belle) tucked her car into the curve of the road to get a closer look. It was a crazy move, but there was no turning back....

A beggar on Main St. with his Manager.

He looked round — an evil leer caught our gaze... Liz instinctively put her foot down —

not a moment too soon. Had she

hesitated we would have been looking down the muzzle of a .44 Garden Hose.

BAGGAGE CLAIM TRANSPORTATION

TEXAS RANGER 1960
TAKE NOT ONE RANGER

Driving out to the hotel 15 miles out of town I was instantly struck by the temporary jerry-built look of the buildings along the highway. Now I'm not one to find fault but everything was frayed at the edges. The Kennedy Memorial which we saw the next day was the only piece of concrete real estate likely to stand the test of time except that it had no roof on it. Right next to it on the Memorial Square was a log cabin – the first home in Dallas, circa 1841. The home of John Newby Bryan. I thought at first it was the first jailhouse until I read the plaque.

The Kennedy Museum was really bringing in the revenue. A film show complete with a model of Dallas, reconstructing the assassination, 20 minutes long, finishing with a flash of light and a bang. Afterwards you are led through a museum of objects and ephemera of the fateful day, complete with the three bullets – two actually – one of them had obviously dropped off the wall at some point, leaving only a glue mark. On leaving the museum you enter the souvenir hall. Counters loaded with memorial pictures, medallions and a reconstruction book by ex-Dallas Police chief Jesse Curry including a photo of the autopsied body of Lee Harvey Oswald.

Brightly coloured postcards of the Book Depository show exactly where the bullets came from and where they went. Just the thing to write home on to news-hungry friends.

Kennedy
Memorial.

Left bank

The Shoe Shine and the Crippled

The RIO GRANDE

Middle American Potwurst . . . sort of a sausage-like form with bulges. Covered in dark, cherry-red, slimy, slick white chequered nylon clothing that doesn't quite contain the contents . . . and white shoes – you've got to wear white shoes – and white skin helps a lot.

It's so difficult for one as disgruntled and uptight as me to become a tourist.

'Be a tourist!' I said. 'Go on – look gaga at everything. Relax. Enjoy the view. Make colour slides you can be justly proud of on those long winter evenings. Delight your friends back home with fun stories. Hire a car and get about.' 'This is no time to relax', I cautioned my wife. 'You are with me to help seek out the bitter truth – not to enjoy yourself. This is an assignment.'

'Your car's out front, sir', said the *Hertz* lady. I moved instinctively towards the mini French Opel. 'No sir, that one's yours', she said, pointing to a monstrous green Ford horror with a front and back like aircraft hangars.

We gave an unusually friendly Texan a lift into town who sat next to me with his baggage against the dashboard and his knees hard against his chest. By the time we reached Santa Fe I had got the hang of the automatic gears and the seasickening roll of the car's suspension.

Although we did not realise it, we had arrived on the weekend of the 52nd Indian Festival. Say no more. We'd see it all. The hotel was perfect. No air conditioning. Just open windows and warm beer. Home from home. The streets were full of temporary stalls strewn with cheap plastic handbags, jewellery made from a variety of materials ranging from turquoise to tin cans, and Indian artefacts like Tomahawks and black Hopi hats and feathers for every occasion. The feather dinner jacket was rather fetching and I was quite taken by the rattlesnake bikini.

Harmonica Player. Tijuana main St. Jan. 84

The Indians were overwhelmingly colourful. 'Keep a steady hand, lad – and a savage eye. It can't be real. Cynical, boy – cynical. This is not the landing of the Pilgrim Fathers.'

Fifteen thousand Middle-Americans jostled to bury their faces into the mounds of turquoise dripping off every other stall. That was what they were there for. The turquoise vultures. Thousands of dollars' worth of the stuff festooning sun-stroked bodies as they try to wear it all at once. Already covered from head to foot, 500 state-controlled Indians urge them to buy more with cries of 'That's for you man, that's just for you!'

I look at a Navajo Bread Wagon for gentle relief . . . Sunday was a day out to meet the really Indian Indians – 60 miles north of Santa Fe on Route 285 to Taos Pueblo, where Adobe houses rise up five storeys in pure mud and straw. Entrance fee – a dollar fifty. 'Oh, you wanna take pictures, sir? That'll be another 2 dollars. Is that a sketch book?' 'Er – yes.' 'You wanna sketch too?' 'Er, yes, of course.' 'That's another five dollars.' 'Oh, I, er, have my oil painting kit with me also. Is that extra?' 'Sure – that's another 25 dollars.'

'HI!' A beautiful little Indian girl sits down on the crossbar of a gate beside me. 'What you doin'?' 'Oh, I'm sketching your beautiful houses. Do you live here?' – 'Uh-huh', she replies. 'You've probably lived here all your life?' 'Uh-huh.'

'Well, you probably take it for granted and wonder why all these people keep coming here just to . . .' 'You wanna take my picture?' 'Well', I reply, delighted – 'I was actually going to ask you – I'd love to.' 'O.K.' She moves away from me and adopts a pose like a totem pole. 'Er, beautiful', click, 'thank you.' I resume my drawing. She comes and sits next to me again. 'You're very friendly.' I continue to draw, trying to make conversation. She moves around me, looks over my page, fidgets, and then braces herself. 'You ain't allowed to take pictures if you don't pay.' 'Oh, but I paid', I said. 'Five dollars to sketch and two dollars to take pictures – even 25 dollars to oil paint.' I resume my drawing uneasily. 'Well, you ain't paid me!' – 'Oh, you, well I thought you came with the price at the gate?' – 'Nope! Children are extra. I'll take a quarter.'

To cool off under the sweltering heat of a late afternoon, we paddle our feet in a small stream littered with Budweiser cans and detergent canisters. Bliss! 'Get your filthy sweating tourist feet out of that sacred water!' An obvious Indian, wearing a seersucker suit and two-tone shoes is bearing down on us brandishing an indoor T.V. aerial. Time to leave.

We don't stop in the town of Taos again on the way out (hello, Dennis Weaver) – we head straight back for Santa Fe – dreams of the noble savage shattered – screwed to his totem by the white man.

Street Vendor

Taos Pue

I THINK WE GOT 'EM SURROUNDED!

PARKING

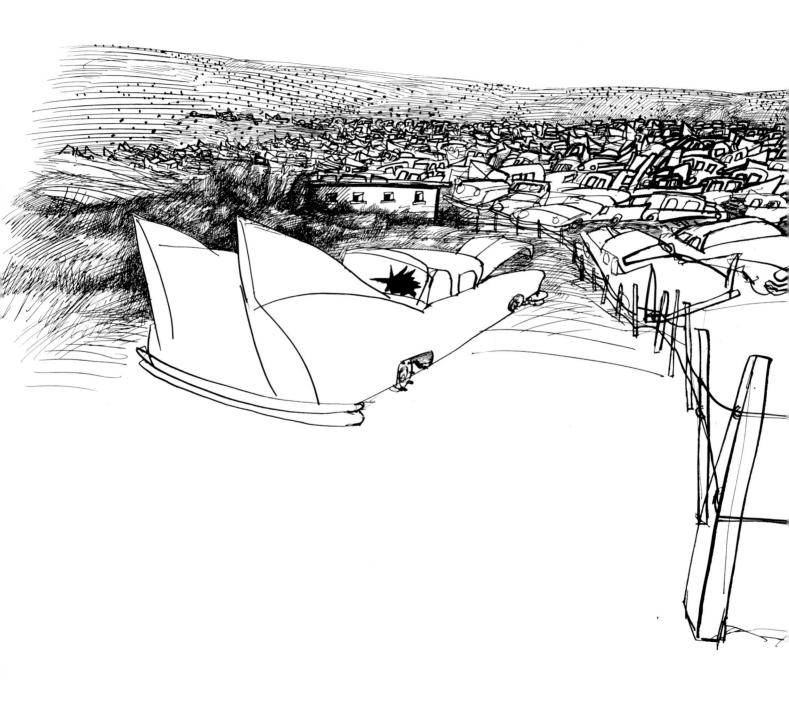

Ralph STEADMAN

Money Changers on the San Ysidro Boulevard north of the Mexican

69
65
5
EY
CHANGE
Joyeria LA
COM
ORO
LA CASA
COMPRAMOS
FABRICANTE
VENTA MAYO
428
del
OMPRA
VEN
169

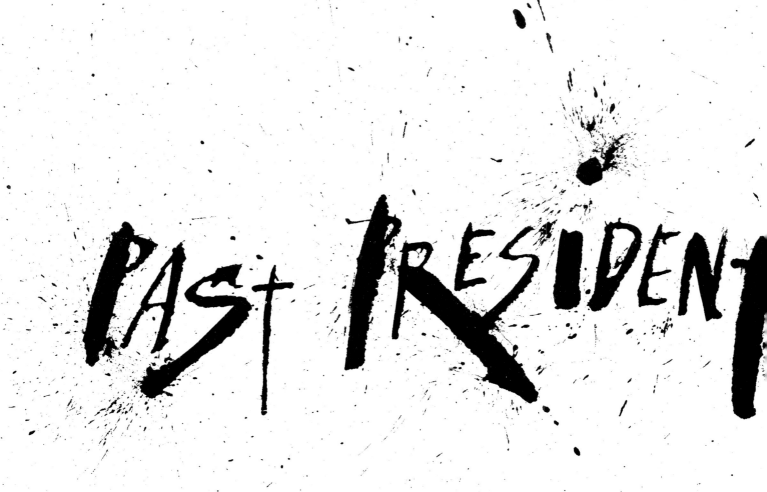

PAST PRESIDENT

Just what kind of President do Americans really want? All voters are individuals and each individual has a very personal idea of just what he expects his President to be.

Someone who had spent 25 years working in a laundromat would have a very different set of criteria for a leader to represent them than, say, a film star. These types have fundamentally different aspirations and they require different things.

A film star, for instance, may be hugely moral and may care more for the plight of the Sandinistas against the might of American foreign policy than the quality of his scripts.

Then again, a laundry worker might have harboured a fetish all his life for dirty politics as a relief from clean underwear, particularly everyone else's. He would quite probably prefer his President to be up to his neck in filth.

You can never tell – and you shouldn't tell. That's how you get people into trouble. Look what happened to poor Mr Nixon – and now poor Mr Reagan. Everybody eager to tell and save their own ass. We are all guilty of something, so keeping quiet is surely a golden rule. Only George Washington told the truth. Abe Lincoln never did, but each in his Machiavellian way achieved his goals.

I do suspect people who want to blurt things out, don't you? It usually means that they are trying to hide something. And all because 'the public ought to know'. A very bad assumption. The less the public know the better, and in fact, the public generally don't know what to do with the time of day whether you give it to them right or wrong. But they *will* ask for it and then say 'oh' blankly. They just need to know. Knowing things makes them feel self-righteous. They suddenly become moral authorities and barrack-room lawyers. They suddenly have opinions they never ever thought of before. But they start by saying, 'I've always thought that – etc', and they give you such a line of heaving bullshit that you'd think they had spent most of their lives in a Trappist monastery, contemplating life.

and FUTURE

I am sure we all realize that we can't get all we hope for out of our leaders. What we really want is a combination of different talents which are not in one human being – a man for all seasons. For instance, lots of people would follow someone who combined the qualities of Richard Nixon and Joan Collins – or even Richard Nixon and Prince Charles. How about Henry Kissinger and J. Edgar Hoover – now there's a thought to bring jam to the boil. Warren Beatty and Geraldine Ferraro, anybody? How about Ronald Reagan and Madonna? For sheer subtlety – Gorbachov and Oliver North.

Of course it's a game, and so it is. The combinations are endless and it makes a harmless enough pastime. It helps to emphasize the fact that nobody's perfect – not even the President – but Americans found that out fifteen years ago. Nevertheless, we all hope that one day we will unearth a real humdinger – someone made of base material, the solid stuff with a touch of Harry Truman, Calvin Coolidge, Abe Lincoln, Salome, and a host of

extras all rolled into one. For whilst America has an extraordinary talent for bubblegum sleaze and chrome-plated hype, they do also have an indestructible hankering for old-time values, the values that sustained the pioneers and farmers of their not-so-distant past. They long to feel substantial behind their junk image. And they *are* substantial, but not so substantial that they can't persistently goof up trying to find a truly great leader. It's really time they went for a woman. My couple of suggestions are obvious ones, because I didn't want to influence anybody, as strong visual puns can. But it's up to America to come up with their own candidates. There must be someone of the fairer sex with the balls to hack it for at least a term. Not an Iron Lady, you understand, but someone with a sense of proportion, a quiet firm manner and a touch of Mother Earth about her.

An utterly flawless soul in our world is an impossibility. To pass through life without impairing or soiling the mind through experience suggests only that the subject of such a condition is not receptive and totally unsuited to leadership of any kind.

Anyone mentally and physically able to clutch and hold the tiniest straw of power will find on his way up that he will encounter an awesome series of temptations that even *I* could not resist. It all seems so simple and, dare I say it, logical at the time one is tempted. Personal gain and immediate gratification are powerful drugs, and even appear as a place of refuge from the day-to-day struggles with which we are confronted. It's called being human.

The great sin is being human in public, particularly in front of media men, or journalists as they like to be called to their faces. Media men or journalists are pure and unsullied. Their opinions and recommendations are printed daily and are sacrosanct. Theirs is the Gospel and they are paid for it too. And so they should be. They guide us and form our opinions. They tell us when things are wrong. They praise the worthy and they castigate the insane. Their training is the cauldron of life. They have seen it all, and they are quick to chide when we stray. They speak from on high and by their actions gain our support for a life they deem fit for us all. We must all be thankful they are there, for without them our world would crumble. We would be helpless and ignorant victims of man's tyranny against himself. They are the Beacon, the example. The hideous example of how we should all conduct our lives. We should all sneak about on a monstrous neighbourhood watch. Suspect everybody. We are all guilty so we are all worth watching, though we are not all newsworthy. But never mind. Think of the nasty little details we can gossip about, and the empty days we can fill with

the colour of mortal spice. Why in fact bother to read about it second-hand when we can train ourselves by a journalist's example to see it for ourselves. What to look for and what to read into it. What to invent and what to emphasize when we retell the juicy bits to a friend. We can compare notes and shuffle the stuff about a bit. Particularly about someone in your neighbourhood who already has a reputation, and especially about someone who is even moderately well-known. It's a wonderful idea. You could ruin their life. What a service to mankind! And if you are really good at it you could get real money for it like the professionals do. It's a job of work like any other. Like a brain surgeon or a nuclear physicist. You have just got to be good at it. Hack it. No half measures. Put the knife right in, up to the hilt, or you are not doing your job properly. Good luck.

THE FIFTY DOLLAR SUIT

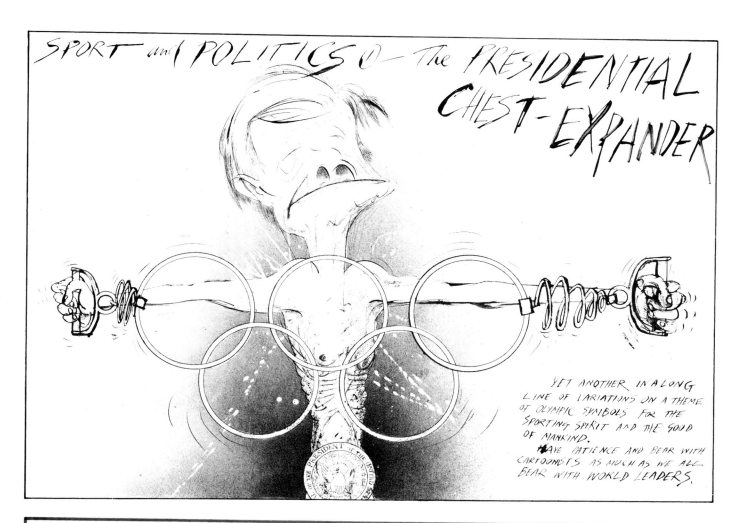

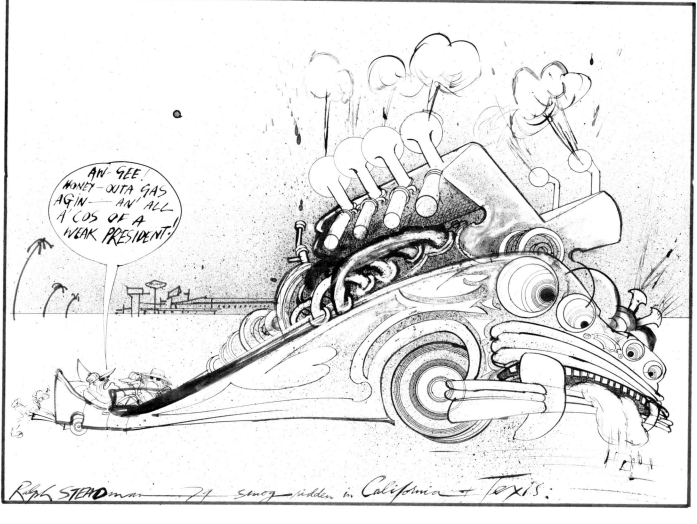

ABE LINCOLN +
Ronald REAGAN.

Ronald REAGAN
+ Gary HART.

Gorbacher +
Oliver NORTH.

Reagan +
Madonna

Ronald REAGAN
& Maggie THATCHER

Maggie THATCHER
& Ronald REAGAN

Ronald REAGAN
& Paul NEWMAN

Richard NIXON
and Joan COLLINS

George WASHINGTON

Henry KISSINGER

Jimmy Carter &
Richard NIXON

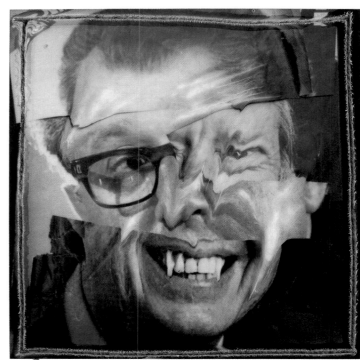

Richard NIXON,
Henry KISSINGER &
Jimmy CARTER

Prince Charles
and Richard NIXON

Woody ALLEN +
Richard NIXON

Henry KISSINGER +
J. Edgar HOOVER

Richard NIXON
+ Ronald REAGAN

Unless it spits blood, it ain't sport. Unless it gathers together the biggest bunch of blood-crazed bone-breakers inside a stadium fit for a Roman Empire to watch gladiators, it ain't sport.

Americans possess an adamantine streak that was forged in their national soul when the Pilgrim Fathers left England in 1620 to worship in their own way. They came to a strange land and prayed with a passion that could not be sustained, for a God they could not see, or might have left behind. Over three centuries that fervour has been transposed into worship for another kind of God: a God of action, a superhero, or, rather, teams of them. An American is born again in a football stadium. His gods move fast and castigate the enemy with a force and power sufficient to live up to, represent, and evoke the force and power of the country itself.

American sport is an outward expression of the country's life-blood, the bursting of a dam, the outpourings of a reservoir of, as yet, untapped energy. The driving force lies deep in the American psyche. Americans live with the certain knowledge that the real source of their greatness has not been released. The intensity of their worship drives the gods in the arena beyond mortal goals and beyond normal brute force, so much so that these gods are encased in armour to ward off evil spirits and the unthinkable possibility that they may be injured, albeit by another god from another place.

I can think of no other explanation for the carnage that Americans demand from their sporting activities or the costumes that they fashion so ingeniously to adorn their gods with. Coupled with their talents for exploitation and big business, such a potent combination is irresistible to the American way. It is all I can say about sport. It is a generous view. It is a view that will not dim their enthusiasm nor the fact that it drew some pretty juicy pictures out of me. There's not that much good sporting art about.

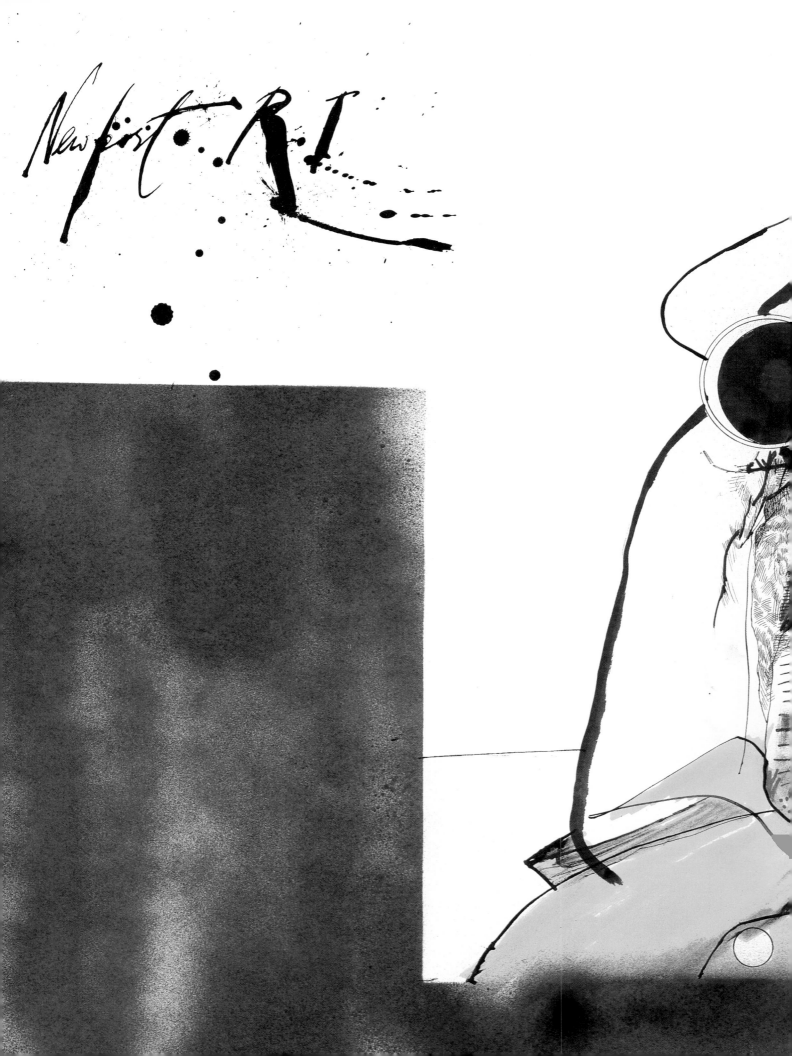

I remember the America's Cup well, the particular America's Cup, the America's Cup of my nightmares and daymares, ugly flashbacks and palpitations, dreamscarred eyes behind pulsing flesh lids, trying to sleep, trying to forget the aftermath of what appeared to start as an intriguing and pleasant week. Dr Hunter S Thompson – ah, yes, life on the ocean, time-honoured codes of seafaring ways, no cares, free, at sea and awash with good buddies for a romp on a fifty-foot sloop, seasick but sod it. This was an assignment and work was the last thing on our minds. The magazine was going down anyway, but the sloop was afloat and we were on it with enough of their money to keep us flying at least until the end of the race, that is if they didn't keep stopping to review the positions of the two racing yachts fighting it out for some kind of advantage on a heaving Atlantic swell. There is no knowing what you do with a nervous captain in charge of two freak journalists and an unknown rock band along for the ego-trip, except maybe ignore him and hope that he understands the irrational behaviour patterns of artists at work. I don't remember how he *did* take the strange downhill turn when I finally overcame my miserable three-day seasickness with a pill that drove me from reasonable consciousness to wild and dribbling vandalism, intent on only one act. An act so unthinkable as to render it impossible. Naturally, the only reason for a sensitive artist to be at the America's Cup at all. With readily available red and black spray cans, it seemed my only mission in life was to write 'Fuck the POPE' on the side of the GRETEL, or maybe it was the INTREPID, what the hell, one or other of the racing boats would do just as well for my painting surface. I wasn't taking sides. I was the artist.

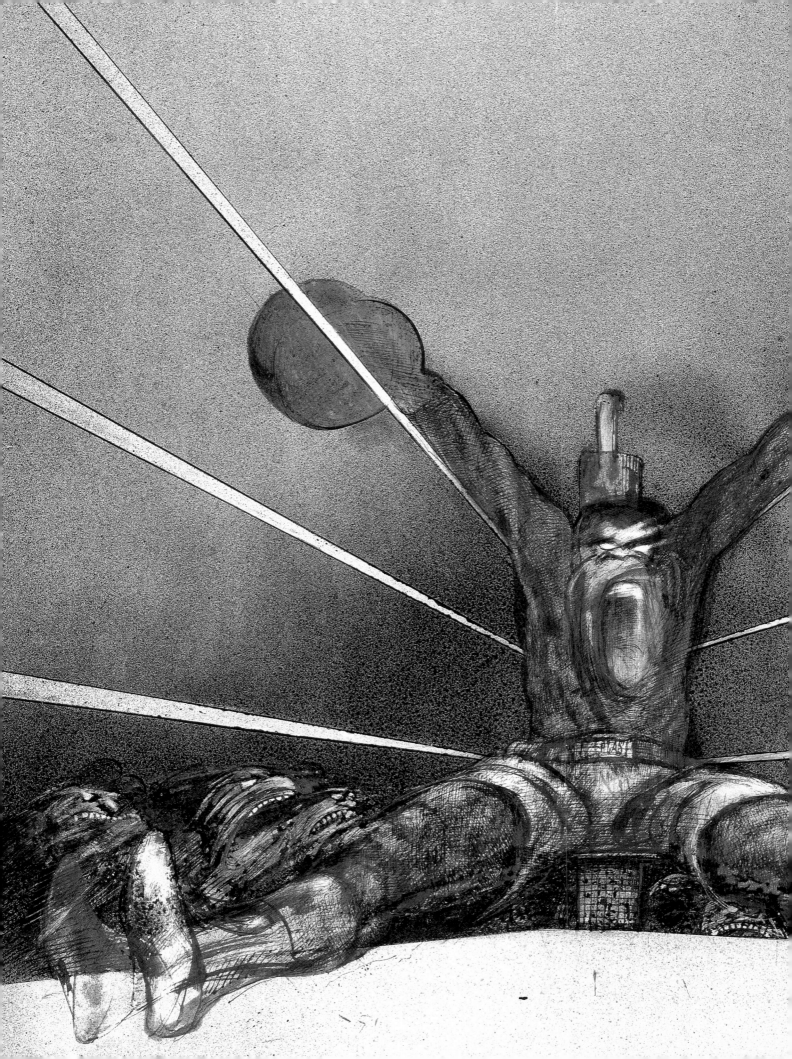

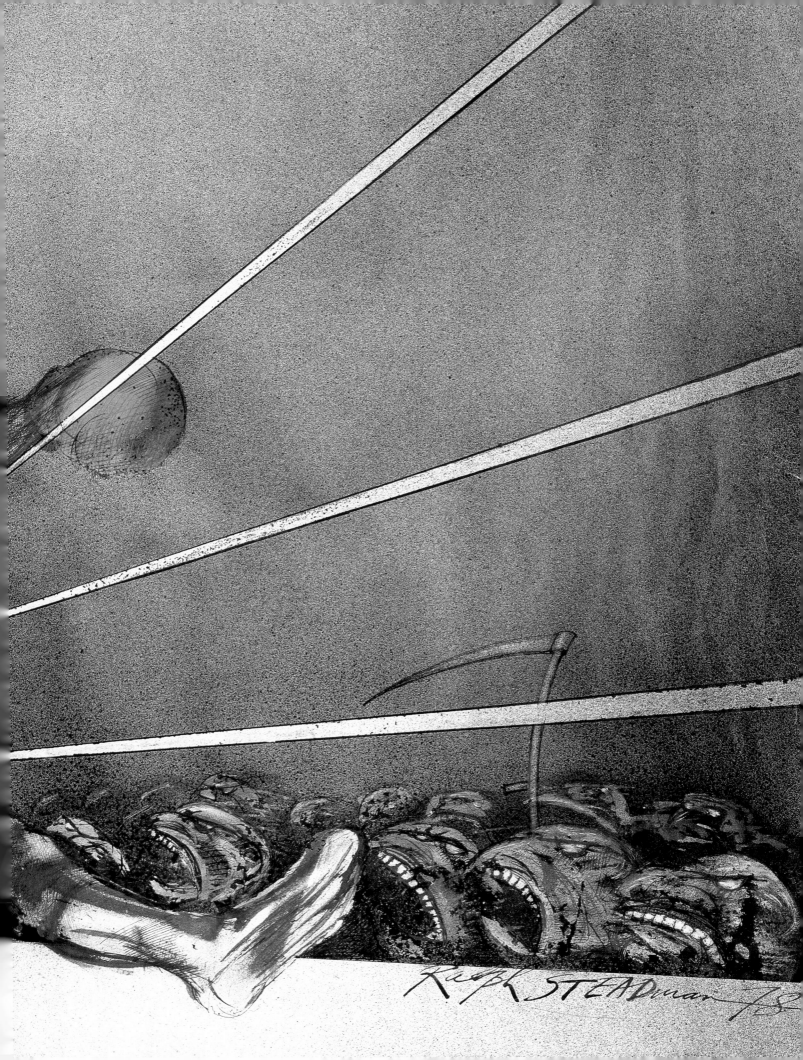

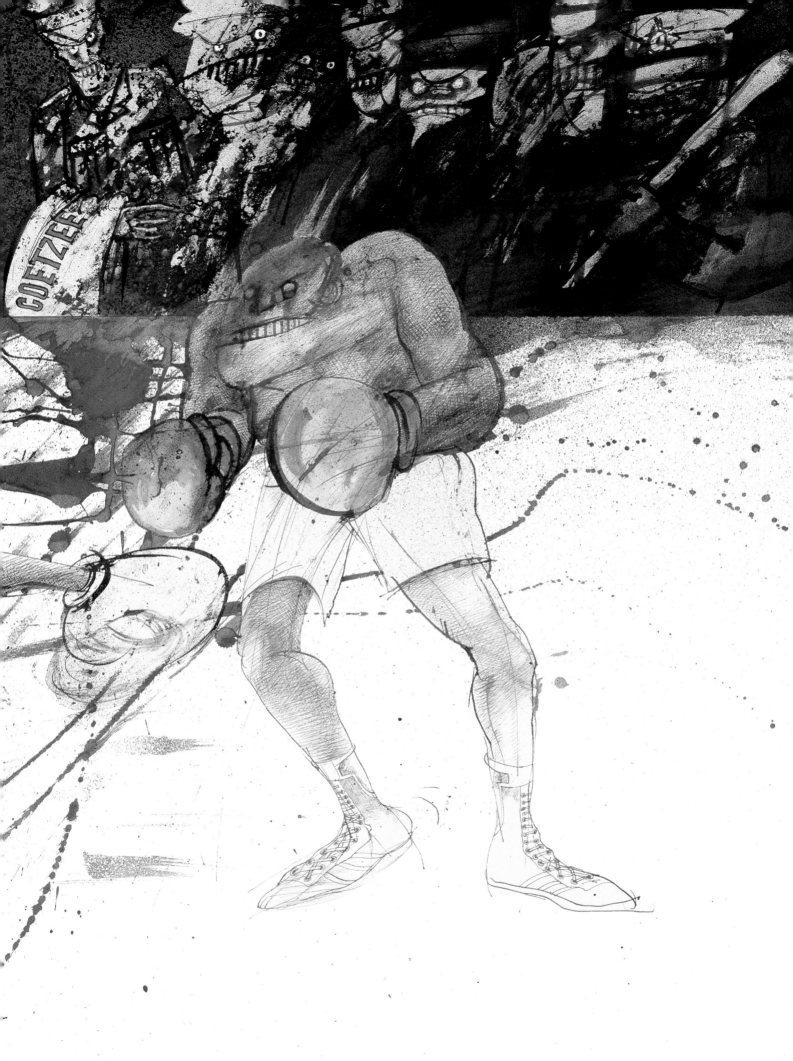

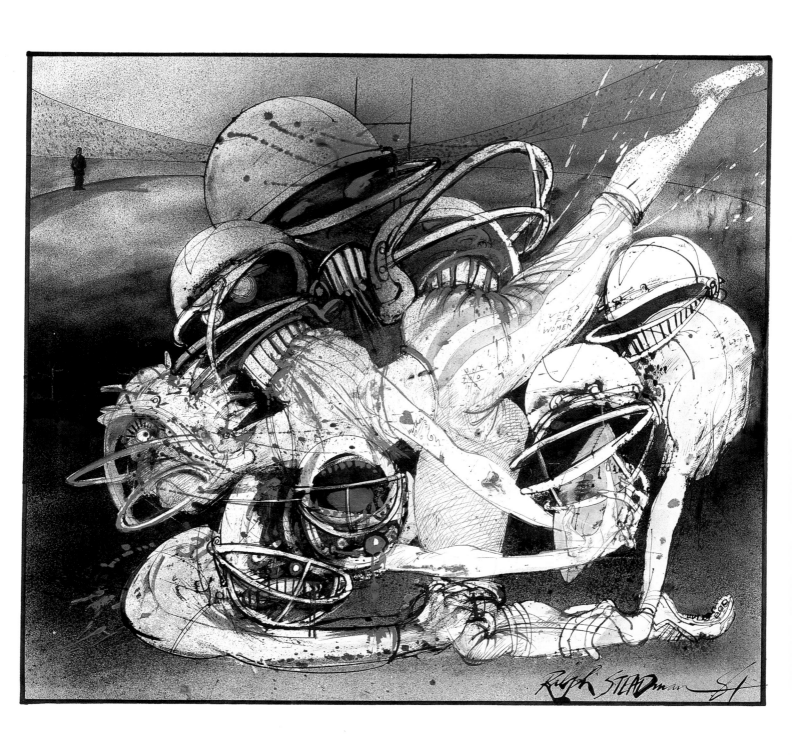

Perish the thought, but I've always thought that if the Pentagon thought they could have got away with it they would have dropped a pile of bombs on Russia years ago. It has been a long-felt desire, since the building of the Berlin Wall. God knows Americans hate Communism with a fearful intensity, and it represents all their very worst nightmares for a future. Even the most rational of Americans will tell you that they fear for 'our' future if ever the 'Commies' got on top of things. Unfortunately, this concept of Russians being barbaric heathen hordes has taken root deep inside the Western psyche, so much so that we all tend to see the 'enemy' through American eyes.

Yet I can't help feeling that the Russian culture, aside from political ideas, must have much more to offer the West in richness and depth than what we choose to call American culture. And we, the European West, have tended to allow ourselves to be fed to the eyeballs with the American variety since the invention of mass production, and mainly

for economic reasons. Nothing for the soul.

There is something hideously repressive about Russia's political ideals, but I would like to think that this view was not really a reflection of the Russian soul. Equally, there is something hideously repressive about America's economic ideals, and I would like to think that this propensity for acquisition was not entirely a reflection of an American's soul. Since I find that I really like quite a lot of them, I am convinced that it cannot be, and I am sure that this is equally true of the Russians.

Perhaps we are all victims of our leaders' pitiful attempts to lead. They have led us to believe that a deadly weapon, 'in the real world', is 'reason', and this reason is what we use to achieve our goal, whatever that may be. Therefore, when our leaders negotiate, what they are actually doing is threatening, depending on who has the biggest reason. So logically, reason has continued to prevail, and will do so until somebody decides that it is time to be unreasonable.

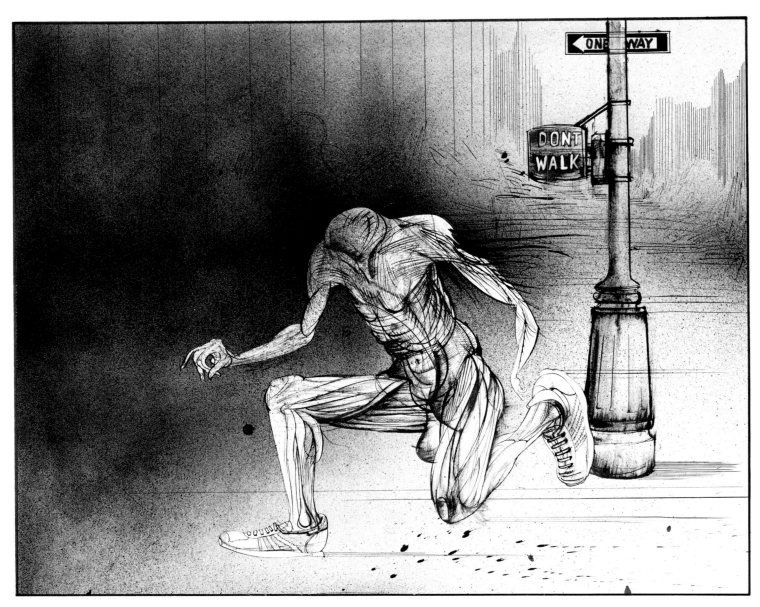

TO OPERATE:
SIMPLY STRANGLE THE
BABY WITH YOUR OWN
BARE HANDS - THEN
PRESS RED BUTTON.

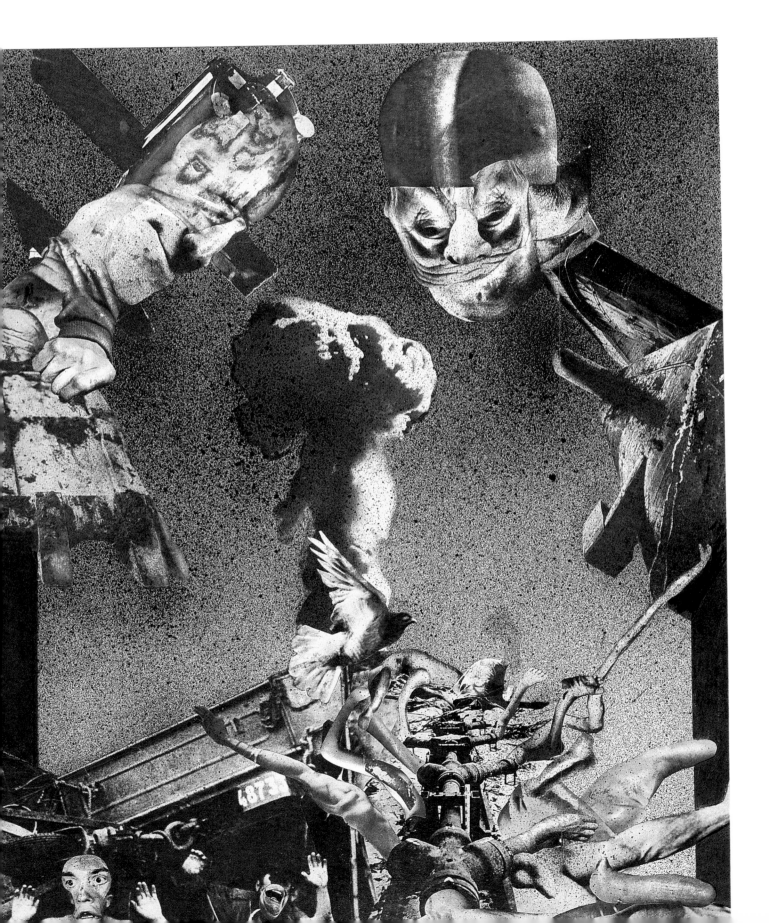

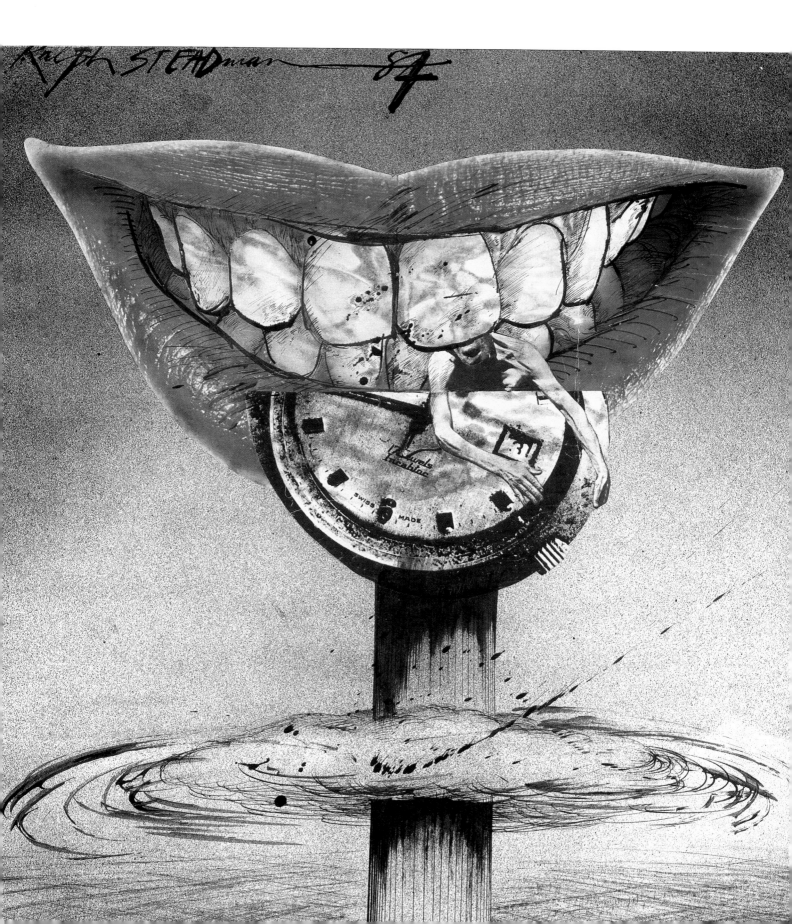

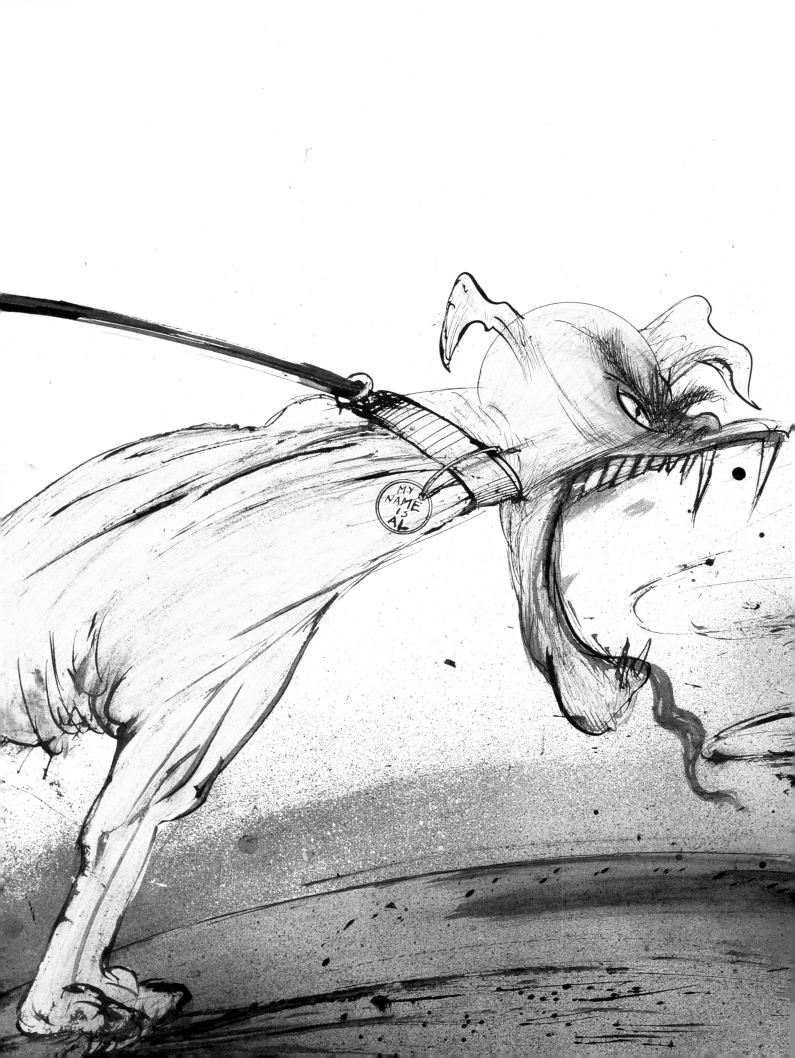

MY NAME IS CASPER

Ralph STEADman

Conventions are campaigns in the ass. They are America's official way of burning candles at both ends. Balloons, ticker tape, Oxford boaters, red, white and blue smiles striped for action, burst into the stratosphere of the convention hall. Bubbling cascades of frothy enthusiasm fill the air, shaming the unconverted into submission. To try and isolate oneself from the effervescent nonsense of it all is like trying to bail water out of a leaky boat in a mid-Atlantic storm.

The first time I encountered one was in 1972, in Miami, when Richard Nixon was in full flight and about to get a landslide victory, with Spiro Agnew as his running mate. Those were still the good old days when a criminal President of the United States was about as unthinkable as forgetting to leave an American flag on the moon on departure.

I was feeling particularly self-righteous and shocked by the raw banality of it all. I felt as though by some terrible mistake I had wandered into the

middle of a riot in some huge ice-cream parlour. I searched in vain for something savoury to touch my pining soul, some hint of common sense to hold on to. There was nothing but this desert of riotous fun and hollow eulogizing from the platform. And most frightening of all, it was a deadly serious display of self-confidence whipped up to fever pitch for the real purpose – to win the election.

The silliness of it all is intended to act as a casual declaration that all is fine and winning is merely a foregone conclusion, which in this case, as it happened, was true with a vengeance. There is no justice in the world. This was the victory of people who were greedy, degenerate (as they most definitely were at that time, or at least blind) and sated with their own sense of rightness. It was a lesson to me never to heed anything my mother ever told me on her knee if I really wanted to succeed in this world. I never forgot the experience or the lessons I learned, though I remained true to myself

and, consequently, still live a life of doubt. The problem was that the experience broke my spirit, and I left two days after I arrived, unable to overcome the nausea that came over me in waves.

I am obviously not a joiner and cannot allow myself what must be an enjoyable thrill – to allow oneself to switch off and become a throbbing part of group abandon. My loss, and I hot-footed it to the airport to catch whatever flight would distance me from that raving melée.

Whilst waiting for the flight, I amused myself with a slot machine which for 25 cents made a brown plastic alligator before your very eyes. I inserted a coin and watched in horror as a filthy brown goo was masticated and squelched into a mould like a weak and uncommitted delegate at the convention I had just fled from. Finally, it was released from the crusher's grip, and, like some newborn featherless creature, it plopped into the receptacle below.

I lifted the cover and took the thing in my hand. It felt sweaty and unhealthy and still a little soft. There was something symbolic about it, and I carefully placed it in the corner of my hand luggage, where it stayed until I got home and set myself down to work. I set it in front of me on my drawing board and drew inspiration from its sickly power. It became my talisman, my voodoo figure and my ally against something which troubles me still.

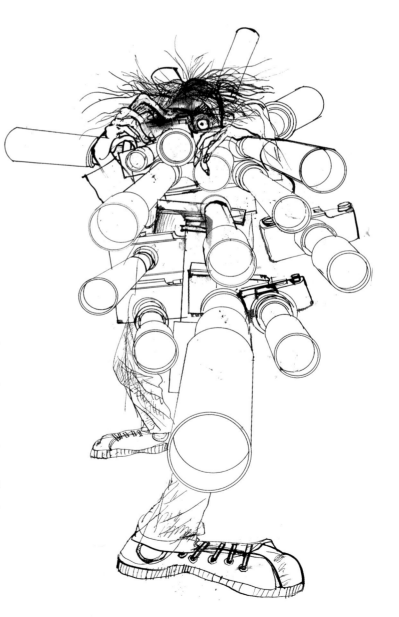

I can only say in defence of my strange reactions that, as things turned out, my instincts were right. Something was wrong. Something was sweaty and unhealthy and sickly about it all. I felt the same in 1976, too, but without the shock value of the first time. Maybe I will always feel it, just so long as you lot remain incurable suckers for the kind of President who promises the earth or manages to convince you that they are really Mother Teresa on a world tour.

What you really need is somebody who is a cross between Abe Lincoln and Woody Allen – but you probably think I'm joking.

REPUBLICAN LADIES
FRIDAY 13 Aug '76

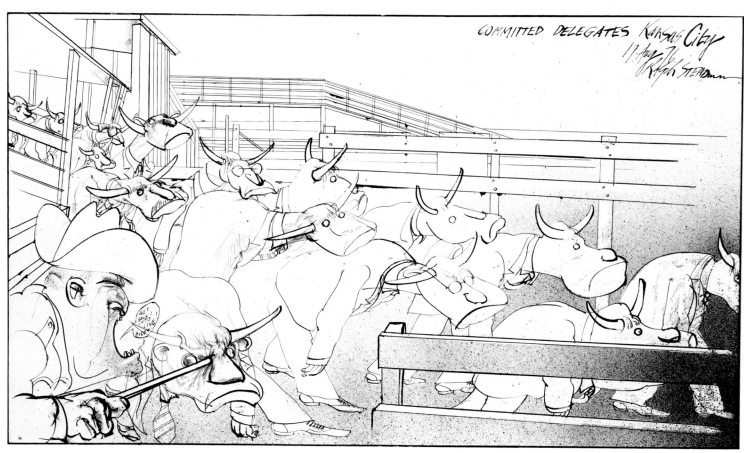

COMMITTED DELEGATES Kansas City
13 Aug 76
Ralph STEADman

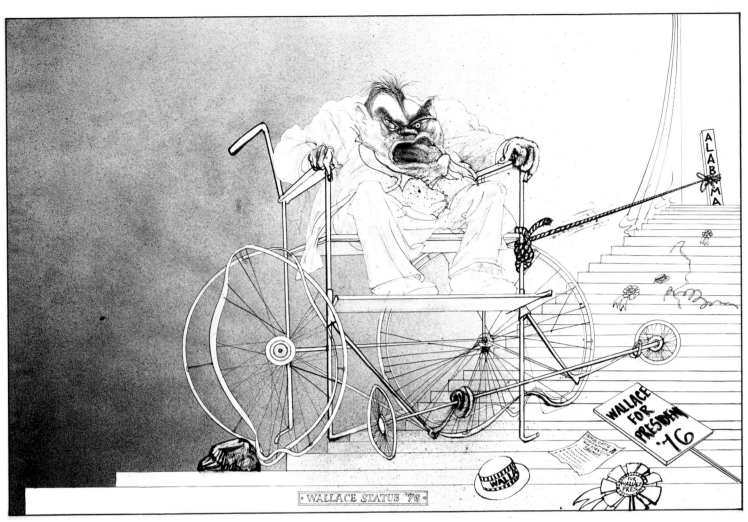

The Dissenters to the Republican nomination arriving at Flamingo Park — veterans of 1 campaign in S.E. Asia.

MIAMI BEACH CONVENTION HALL

VIETNAM VETERANS AGAINST THE WAR CALIFORNIA.

AN AVERAGE MATURE AMERICAN HAVING BEEN TOLD THE GOOD NEWS THAT HE HAS GAINED THE REPUBLICAN PRESIDENTIAL NOMINATION, NOW HEARING THE BAD NEWS THAT THE SENATE SELECT COMMITTEE INVESTIGATING IRANSCAM REQUIRE HIS ATTENDANCE AT HEARINGS TO ANSWER QUESTIONS REGARDING HIS POSSIBLE INVOLVEMENT IN THE CHANNELING OF FUNDS THROUGH UNDISCLOSED SWISS AND PANAMANIAN BANK ACCOUNTS.....

HE IS ABOUT TO INVOKE THE FIFTH AMENDMENT

SEAL OF THE PRESIDENT OF THE UNITED STATES

IN

OUT

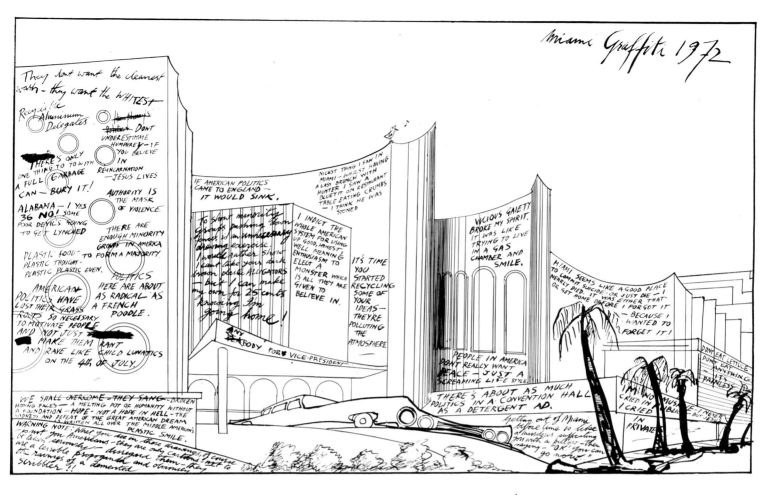

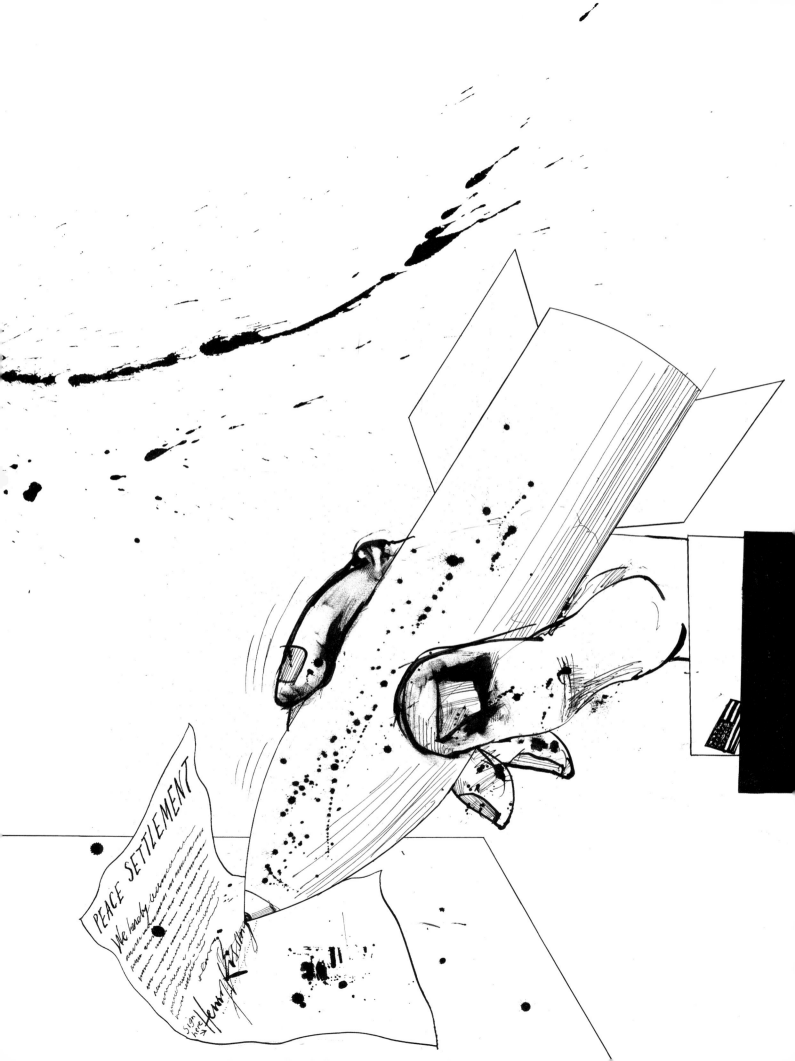

It is clear to everyone
that the suicide of civilization
is in progress.
Wherever there is lost
the consciousness that every man
is an object of concern for us
just because he is a man,
civilization and morals are shaken
and the advance to truly
developed inhumanity is only
a question of time.

Albert Schweitzer
THE PHILOSOPHY OF CIVILIZATION

The PRICE OF MEAT!

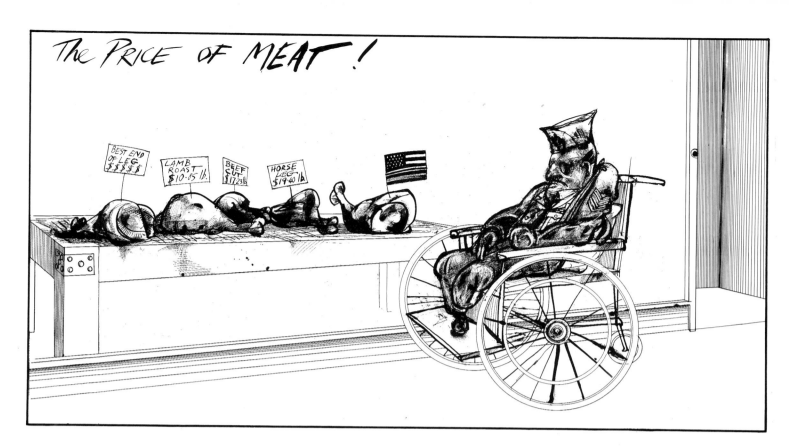

THE WARRIOR'S RETURN.

AIDS is the biggest thing since the Wall Street Crash (with the possible exception of the Vietnam War). It has America mouthing sentiments that ten years earlier it would not have been seen dead uttering. Small wonder, but nevertheless alarming.

Suddenly it is respectable to be a bigot. Suddenly, the social freedoms gained so magnificently since the 1950's are being hastily transformed into moral cancers, and a determined ostracisation of the unclean is underway. A whole society is busily distancing itself from any contaminating possibilities and scrambling to beat an undignified retreat inside the walls of a fortress of purity, reminiscent of the behaviour of the characters in Edgar Allen Poe's *Masque of the Red Death*. It was no cure in the story, anymore than it was a cure for the thousands who could afford to flee from the Black Death of 1348, a little before America's time. They blamed the rats and the rats blamed the fleas who carried the bubonic virus. There is a Nobel Prize in prospect, if not a canonisation, for the inventor of a genuine cure for AIDS, not to mention riches beyond the dreams of Texans, and no doubt it will come. Probably something as simple as the green mould that forms on an undrunk glass of Coca-Cola (must check that out!) or the froth that forms around the mouth of a dog who just tried to eat a frog. It will be found. My latter suggestion is probably the one. Apportioning blame has become a popular sport of the Eighties, the decade of the self-righteous. Out of the woodwork have crawled the pure of mind, mainlining their rancid little thoughts into our

consciousness, as though they have just thought of them. How the hell can you blame any creature on this earth on moral grounds for something which is as much a mystery and a miracle as the meaning of life itself? Accusations of that sort are merely puny opinions of a tawdry mind in the face of the sheer omnipotence of it all.

And when they find a cure, and everything's OK again, what then? Apart from the relief. Will we turn upside down again, will we push our new-found goodness out in a leaky boat and get back to the real business of life, the wondrous hell of it all, one Sodom and Gomorrah of a new age – pure, unadulterated gratification and self-indulgence. Can't you just imagine it?

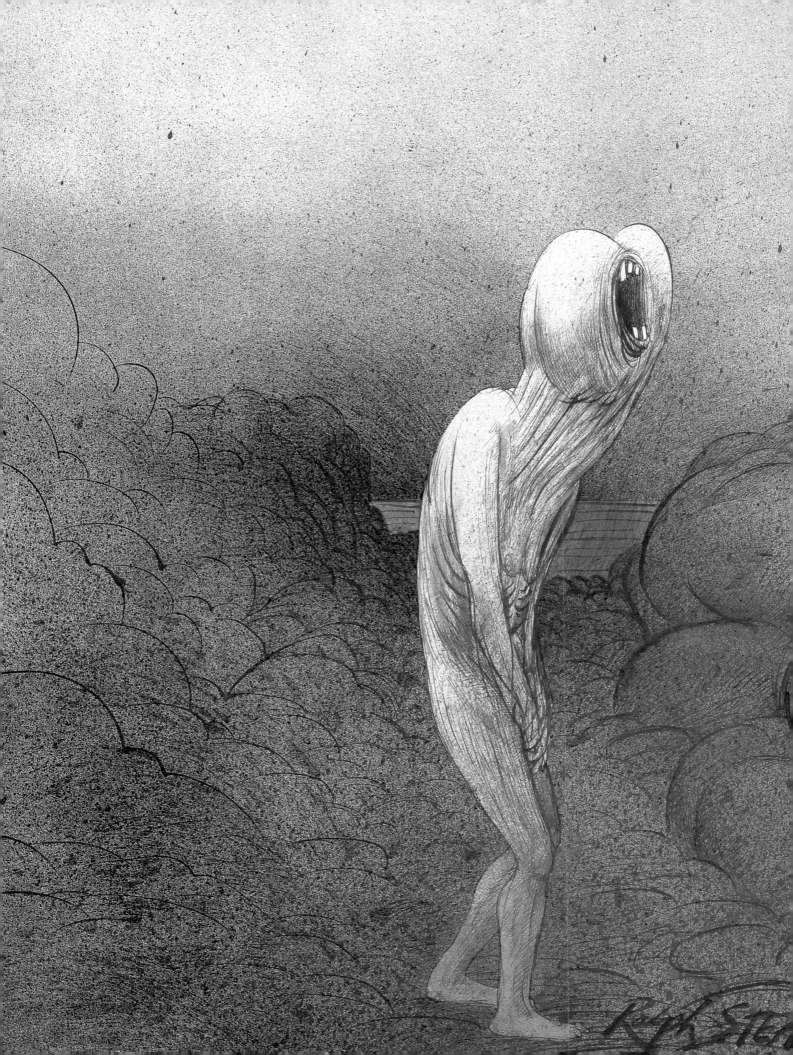

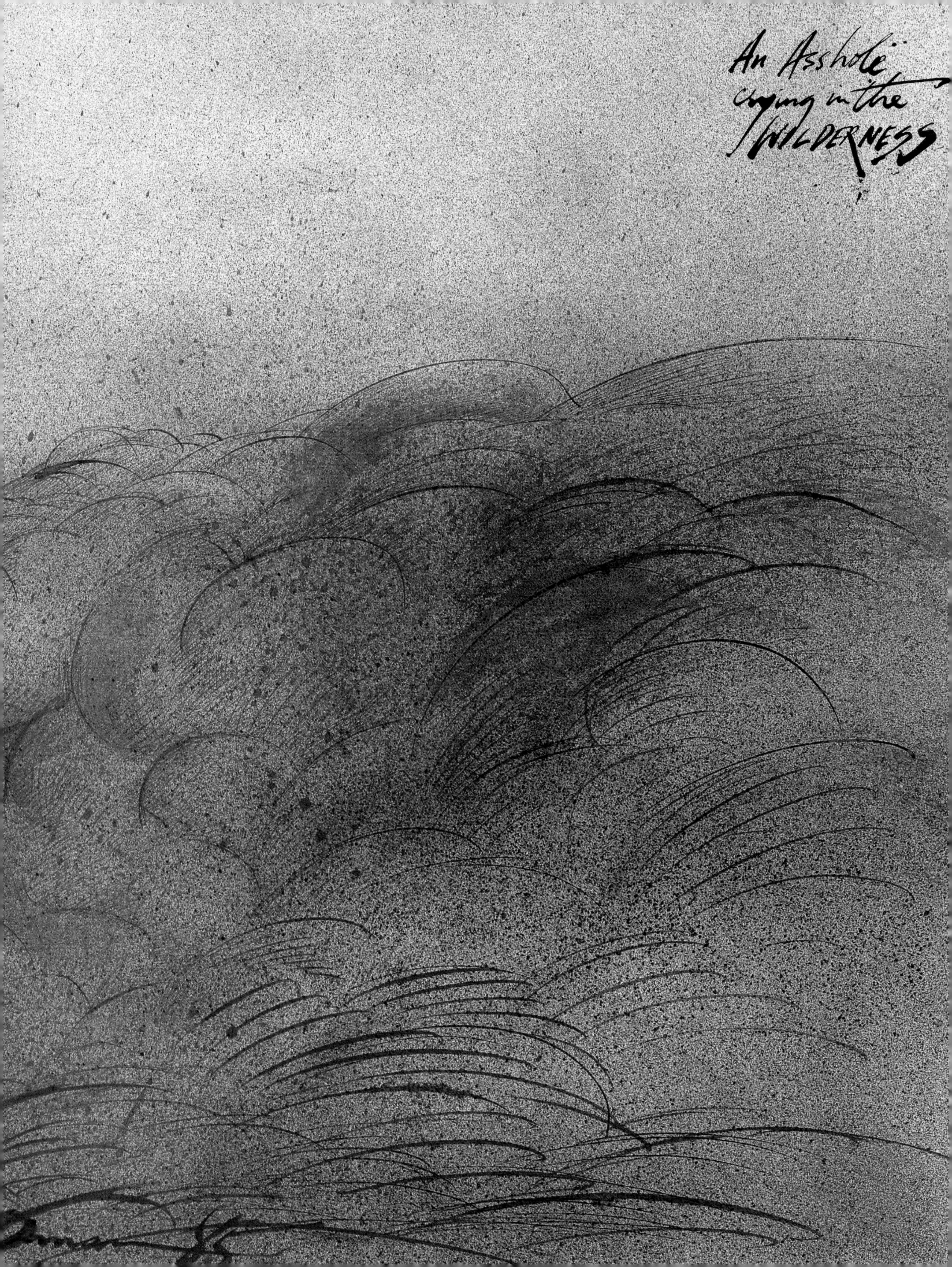

An Asshole
crying in the
WILDERNESS

I suppose it would not be unfair to say that the American nation has been exercising a form of foreign policy ever since the first settlers began to push westward into the north-west territory of Kentucky and Tennessee, making spurious deals with the Indians and worthless treaties to confuse the indigenous populations. But since that was considered 'home' to the new hordes from foreign lands, who had staked their all into this new venture, anything was fair. The Machiavellian principle that the end justified the means was in full swing. The important thing was to win. There was no turning back and therefore desperation was the key word. Them or us. 'Warlike Christian men' were called for to come forward and take up offers of 'Donation Lands' if they had got the guts to take on the Indians and tame the wilderness. It was all foreign policy at the time and, apart from a spate of nineteenth-century presidents who eschewed the idea of getting involved in 'foreign entanglements', the Americans have been at it ever since. With the rise of Communism as the antithesis of all that America stands for, and the progenitor of all her darkest and inexplicable fears, she has set herself up as the bastion for good in the world. She sees her role as the alternative to the Red Threat. In God she trusts and in God they don't.

The West tends to stand behind her and regard her as the sole administrator of such an attitude, and over three-quarters of a century we have come to

accept what is, after all, only a geographic definition. It does not by a long chalk encompass all our attitudes to life as each of us sees it as individuals. Our leaders, in their desperate attempts to be recognized as 'allies', have sold us down the river to a common policy, 'them' and 'us'. The wretched policy of misunderstanding. The policy that disallows our right to 'get to know' the 'opposition'.

Half the American people rebelled against these foreign policies during the Vietnam years and divided a nation. That alone should have been a sign, but obviously the sacrifice was not enough. The powers that be deem it necessary, if only to save face, that the policy of anti-Communism be maintained for the good of us all. *That* surely is a

formula for continued antagonism in a world already stricken with a fear it cannot explain. Yet the fear is the fear of not knowing who 'they' are. We deny ourselves the opportunity of finding out in case we discover that what we are looking at is the face in the driving-mirror.

The energies of all our governments are being used up in the futile pursuit of an impossible goal. There will be no equilibrium whilst there is suspicion and fear. What is exchanged at a summit meeting will be nothing more than the cant of frightened men appearing to represent how the rest of us feel. We will be misrepresented, and the only people who win are arms dealers and government agents whose only task in life is to look employed.

It is a twisted irony that Richard Milhous Nixon turned out to be the one president who understood the need for open confrontation, and who pledged his better self to go to China and meet the people in a way that disarmed a nation sufficiently to enable it to bare its soul and set aside its previous distrust. Maybe the time was right, but maybe he really knew that and went for it. In government now, a handshake is a bear trap, and 'they' are not people like us who think and feel.

Politicians will not realise that the people they claim to represent are really enjoying life whilst it still exists, for it is a pleasant way to go from birth to death. We don't want to fight. We long for the opportunity to trust and learn. Instead, we, the people, are used as the justification for the muscle-

Prisoners of War. GRANADA Oct. 83

flexing postures of those who seem to have set themselves up as arbiters of our wishes.

'Foreign policy' is no more than a device to justify a massive arms budget and a NATO alliance that imposes missile sites and 'defence forces' on countries whose people have no use for them. The trick is to sell the notion that the only way out of this impasse of escalating arms build-up is to preach multilateral disarmament. All one country needs to do is to declare unilateral denial of arms as a solution, and so many others would follow suit.

I have never met a single soul in my entire life who ever wanted their own personal missile in their own back garden, so where are these people who seem to need them? Only those surely who are likely to make money from creating the need.

A MESSAGE of HOPE for 1984

Dateline: I am January 1st 1984
(A TOME of HOPE)

Eagles Nest
BEVERLY HILL
CALIFORNIA.
(on Barcham Green
Handmade Paper)

In the cold light of a curdled dawn . . . . I laughed.

The craven blasphemy could not sustain another day. The year is upon us and it will be magnificent. Believe it. I'm sick of whiners. Crave for Hell, you puerile mentors. I've listened to the disbelievers too long – the thought-hoodlums who cripple hope for this cursed year. Perish the Orwellian nightmare-mongers and banish the brain-grinders. Leave them to their sleazy halfworld – or let them join us. Scrape off the turgid barnacles of dismal failure and enter the New Year as a liberator. The passage of time is not there for us to reason why, but to use. It enjoys perfect rhythm – and so should you.

A cripple will learn to walk on his hands, and he who stands and watches others struggle is doomed to crawl in his own tarnished parade.

Allow me to continue . . . Gather up your loins and crush the barriers that freedom uses to punish its young. Increase in yourselves the belief that there is no Third World. We are all part of a greater community. The grime-wizened old stoop with the empty begging-bowl is your grandmother. There are no rats. No sleek persuaders who wait to eat your brain. Be wise. A timely warning is all that I need offer. I am the red light that stops you at the crossroads. Listen through the music of your car engine. Hear the wheels upon the road. They are where you are going. You with your hand forever in the micro-wave oven! Cut it off and cook it for your neighbour.

1984 is not a witch's cauldron. Those are bubbles of inspiration you see rising to the surface. Throw yourself into the year with confidence. There will be no human soup. Bathe in the rich sauces of mankind's Jacuzzi of abilities. There are no losers. Only BIG BROTHER – unless he joins us instead of merely watching. DOUBLESPEAK is a forked tongue – you can state your truth in half that time and win the Olympic Pole Vault of life. That is not mist you see on your horizon but the doubt of others – hanging in mid-air – or could it be a multitude of white dinosaurs who have lost their way . . .?

11.59 p.m. 31st December 1983

Explanation: Keeping hot bats requires some unconventional wisdom.

'Let your love be like a credit card that you may draw on it all the days of your life.' (TV Evangelist blessing).

Strange days flowing backwards in search of some old-time belief — old-time hoodwink. Clutching the air, reaching out to touch an image of themselves on some higher plane. Like babies on their backs clutching at phantom shapes above their perambulator, a newborn sight, stimulating senses, they struggle to stand themselves up. Flailing helplessly, babies are not perturbed. No sense of failure crosses *their* minds. Theirs is a joyful, learning experience. Their time is coming.

Not so to be born again. Their time is going. They flail like drowning puppies approaching a waterfall, wailing approval towards a demi-god's cant and revivalist hype, who brings the idea of Christ to the market-place for personal gain. These demi-gods know which nerve to prod with the unerring accuracy of a heat-seeking missile. Their sheer puerility lends them a dangerous power. Their repetitive simplicity persuades those who follow not to think. Not to reason. Blessed relief.

Warm, wonderful, blessed imbecility, uniting with others and gaining strength inside a blank communal mind. A state of euphoria overcomes resistance and the struggling victims do drown, drawn under with the dark current of emotional subterfuge.

It's more to do with what we, all of us, want to believe than what we know to be true. Fundamen-

Tammy BAKKER

Jim Bakker.

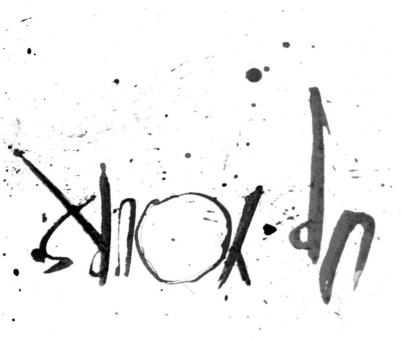

God's telephone number broadcast into people's homes across the nation. Ring now for immediate salvation. All you need to know is your credit-card number. Simply believe, and you are saved from eternal damnation. It's a miracle. An absolute snip. A born-again bargain.

Mining a bottomless pit of latent emotions and dormant tragedies, these believers are easy fodder for the fast-talking, self-deified manipulators of dream-box religion. And it's not just your money they are after. Whilst bringing tears of self-pity to the pleading eyes of the faithful, they are gathering the support of millions as easily as picking cherries, for a far more sinister motive than the founding of personal fortunes and the building of holy Disneylands for the truly pious.

Rabid right-wing Republicanism is on the move with a vengeance, driven by these powerful new generators of public support, confident in the belief that might is right and God the product is on their side. Having scooped up the faith of the wandering masses and hooked them to a sense of spiritual purpose, the party is poised to pull off the

talism reeks of frightened souls; desperate, lost people with a desperate need to believe in something specific to fill the vacuum. Willing to pay for it, turning their 'born again' assumption that the Bible is right, word for word, into something concrete, a perfect transaction. Their souls are bought for real money in God's market-place. This they understand. Salvation costs.

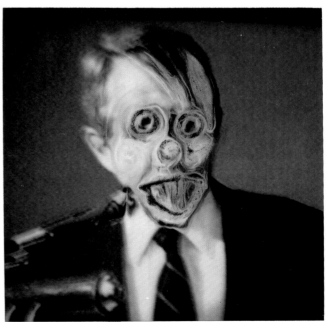

biggest trick in the history of American politics. A vote for the Republicans is a vote for Christ. And the rest – the lefties, homosexuals, junkies, anti-nukes, peace freaks, Nobel Prize winners, moderates, and any other awkward minorities – blacks and Jews included – the rest of us, the minority-majority who happen to have other ideas, well, it's all quite simple, the rest of us can go to Hell.

The new Aryans are coming and vengeance is theirs. No mercy for those who are different. Old-time religion is back in business, and Jesus Christ, if he said anything at all, never said nothing like this to nobody nohow. The tragedy is, it doesn't matter what he said, or how simply he said it. How we choose to interpret it is what counts. Give a hatchet to one person and they will go and chop firewood with it; give it to someone else and they'll hack you to bits. It's all a matter of priorities.

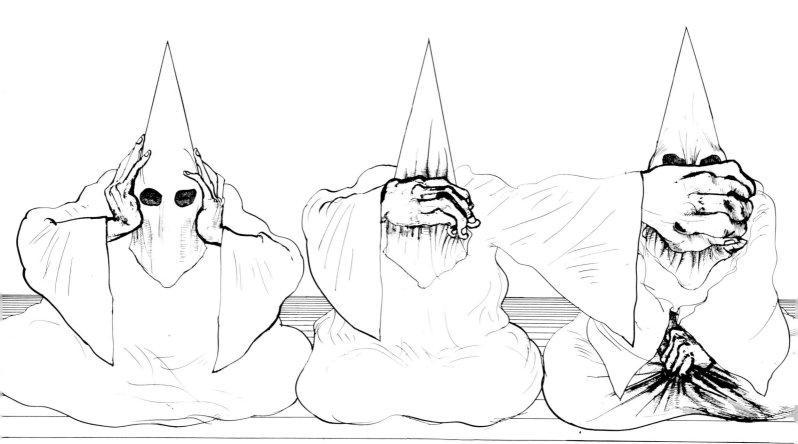

America

We sit petrified, having bought tickets for eleven rides. We've got to go on them, otherwise we haven't done Disneyland; and, anyway, it's a waste of money if you don't use them. But I *am* looking forward to Mr Toad's Wild Ride. Anyway, let's start . . . First stop, Sleeping Beauty's Castle . . .

It's all over, and I'm thrilled about one thing – most people love to do what I hate, like shoving and pushing to get a Wild West Burger, queuing for an hour to get on a Matterhorn bobsled and preferring Autopia to walking through the way-out turnstile.

But imagine the horror when we realised you couldn't get a beer in the whole damn phantasmagoria – just Coke, coffee or lemon tea. That shortened our chances of staying the course to something like 11 to 7.

But in a fine British way we stuck at it, and, somewhere in all that hot, sweaty, composition-building-complex and phoney jungle, something felt good – it may just have been familiar old Mickey. I would have liked it even less if he hadn't been there.

Writing or drawing things down is a desperate situation: nerves are fraught – caught – where's

my notebook? – fuck I've lost it – oh where is it? oh my god no – I'll look again – it must be here. Here! In this bag – Where did you have it last? – In my hand – I think. No – not that stupid bar – Ye Olde Pub . . . all those people – hearing my English voice – no barman – thirsty – five minutes before this bar. Where's the goddamn barman? Pour my own, that's OK – No one will come – Someone's emptied the Watney's barrel already. Pull tap – fake – nothing happens. Ah, here you are, OK. Instead of a Watney's I'll take a Michelob! Thank you – Thank you, sir. Have a nice day! Six in the evening and he's saying "Have a nice day!" Where's that notebook? Must write it down.

Gradually, the circus of people clamouring for canned amusement took on the real spirit of Disneyland '76. We held back, horrified. It seemed the next best thing to having a polythene bag pulled down hard over your sweating head.

The more cosseted we are from the reality of what it is we are doing, the less we experience. But we do experience new feelings and sensations in all these innovations, unreal as they feel in the first moments.

Where's my Mickey Mouse?

Since we live in the age of the third-rate, and surf on the crest of vulgarity's own tidal wave, it is only right and proper to document the greatest, sprawling monument to a mutant culture before it blows away or falls down as it is most certainly meant to.

I remember with affection and awe a sight I have seen many times from a poolside perch of a friend's house high up on the crazy slopes of Beverly Hills. As the evening sun casts orange-black shadows through the haze of a hot landscape, a strange flat purple shroud reveals itself – a hovering, silent menace of petrochemical smog. Angelenos are almost proud of it. It has been there so long. The smog to Los Angeles is what the pyramids are to Egypt. Ominously beautiful, it unites 4,683 square miles of startling contrast and watches over a populous wreaking rich and wretched poor whose greatest industry spins dreams for the whole world and whose excesses spew out of the film sets and on to the streets, reassembling themselves like scenery in an animated cartoon.

I am a stranger in this papier-mâché world, but I feel its plastic heartbeat and I can see its blood glow in neon tubes. I see also its huge joke and I laugh, but to myself, for I know it is somebody's religion and must be recognized as such.

The essence of this culture is the speed with which it can erect its icons and reinvent itself daily. To be unreal is to acknowledge its cardinal rule: anything is possible.

They have built the Tower of Babel up to Heaven – sideways – and they are crossing the desert in a bid to reach Hell.

Conventional good taste does not startle and therefore has no place here. Within its own context it does not need to concern itself with good or bad taste, but simply flavours of the month. Wildness

the RAT

rules, and craves a wilder theme to pump its own adrenalin. Life must be up. There is no time for reflection.

Everything erected has a purpose and must state its case like an exploding bomb if it is to survive. It must be quick, or tomorrow it will be something else entirely.

Three kinds of creatures live best in Los Angeles – crazy people, cockroaches and rats and they all must live somewhere.

Inside the hollow caverns of monstrous brown donuts, winsome cartoon characters and plaster-bound, square-jawed hamburger-eaters lurk the refugees from the sterilized world of breakfast coffee-shops, brunch-joints and cool, dark cocktail-bars down below. It's the only place left for them to go and if they can't make it to the desert they must be content to live in these bizarre hidey-holes with front doors that glow with good news neon messages, declaring the best Mexican tacos, all-nite massage, 365-day laundromat and Christ is Risen. Out of sight and out of mind they would not dare to rub shoulders with the creatures on two legs who use tactics not unlike their own but with far more ruthless cunning.

Life down below is lived at a desperate pitch that would leave the average rat steaming like an old horse and a cockroach choking on its back.

There is laughter, of course, but it rises to cackling fever pitch at the sound of cascading money too many times a day, and that means nothing to a rat.

The instant and the new are the vital mainsprings that have created an art form with no roots in the sand, no rules and an aesthetic yardstick forged only by the power of what it has to sell. But it all had to start somehow, and while the endless stream of pioneer sod-busters who left Independence,

Missouri, in the early 1840's, and made it finally to the Pacific West, didn't actually start this trend in tackiness and technicolour bawd, they may have sown those early seeds of the line.

They were, after all, eager, desperate souls, hungry for land and prosperity, otherwise they would never have attempted such a trek in the first place. They must have been acquisitive and prepared to suffer hellish privations and try anything that worked which could be construed as a sterling quality, whatever it finally wrought, though they can hardly be blamed directly for the Disneyland that grew up by the name of Los Angeles.

They were in search of the fertile earthly paradise, the God-given reward for pitting their courage against the wilderness.

Instead, they found a desert with little or no water, which is no problem at all if you know where to look for it, and if you have just travelled 2,000 miles and crossed some of the greatest rivers, you'd know where to look. So they tapped the Colorado river with a big pipe 300 miles long and behold a Fertile Earthly Paradise was born. With near-tropical weather and limitless water on tap the place sprouted like an Amazonian jungle.

With the coming of the huddled masses, the discovery of oil, the invention of the internal combustion engine and cinematography, instant prosperity and the wildest of dreams were realized with the speed which the Angelenos have not made the slightest effort to stem to this day.

Today the place screams like a punkish whore bedecked with more layers of fluorescent colour and chrome-plated kitch than a monster Wurlitzer.

Its shape owes nothing to any ideal but its own. If you are selling hotdogs then that is the perfect shape for a building and it tells the masses outside exactly what you are selling so you don't waste their time. It is the most logical mainline communication system yet devised. All you need to know from an architect, if that's what you would call him, is whether the damn thing will stay up long enough to make a fast buck and get the hell out before the last customer has even spread his ketchup.

I forgive it all because it is so brutal and so honest and perhaps most because it is so like itself. I even respect it in a certain way, as I respect a cobra or a killer whale.

I don't want to live in it, buy it or write a sonnet on the banks of its flowing freeways. I see no romance in the poolside scenery, no substance in the stupored lives of suntanned figures in a landscape; take no comfort from the frantic services offered around the clock, feel no warmth in the glow of a liquor-store window in the early hours, nor do I shudder with delight at this screaming lifestyle. Then maybe I'm already gone. The victim of a glittering drug strewn along a thousand miles of sidewalk. A lousy B-movie actor who struts and frets his hour upon a tacky film set, and then is heard no more.

But the tale he had to tell, if only he'd had the chance, is already scrawled in swash-buckling neon letters on children's building blocks anywhere you care to look — by the devil's Poet Laureate himself in the kingdom of the blind where the one-eyed man wears shades and drives a white Cadillac.

Money is money. Money is life. Money swears. Money is the lowest common denominator in the highest common cause. Money outstrips our best intentions. Money gives us new morals and new ideas when it flows. Money buys happiness, health, long life and souls. Money smothers problems and money divides the wheat from the chaff. Money murders. Money makes manners and

money decides how we should behave. Money shapes our societies, and no matter how strong we think we are, and how committed to an idea we may be, money can buy it lock, stock and barrel. Money can make you believe that black is white, bad is good, and shit is edible, and I ought to know because I just ate some.

Money is $$$ and sometimes $$$$$$$$$$$$$ $$$$$$$$$$$$$$$$$$$$$$$$$$$$$$$$$$$$

$$$ but more often than not it is $$ though occasionally it is $$$$$$$$$$$$$$$$$$$$$$$$$$$$$$ $$$$$$$$$$$$$$$$$$$ and $$$$$$$$$$$$$$$$$$$ $$$.

It will always $$$ and never let you $$$ except in certain circumstances.

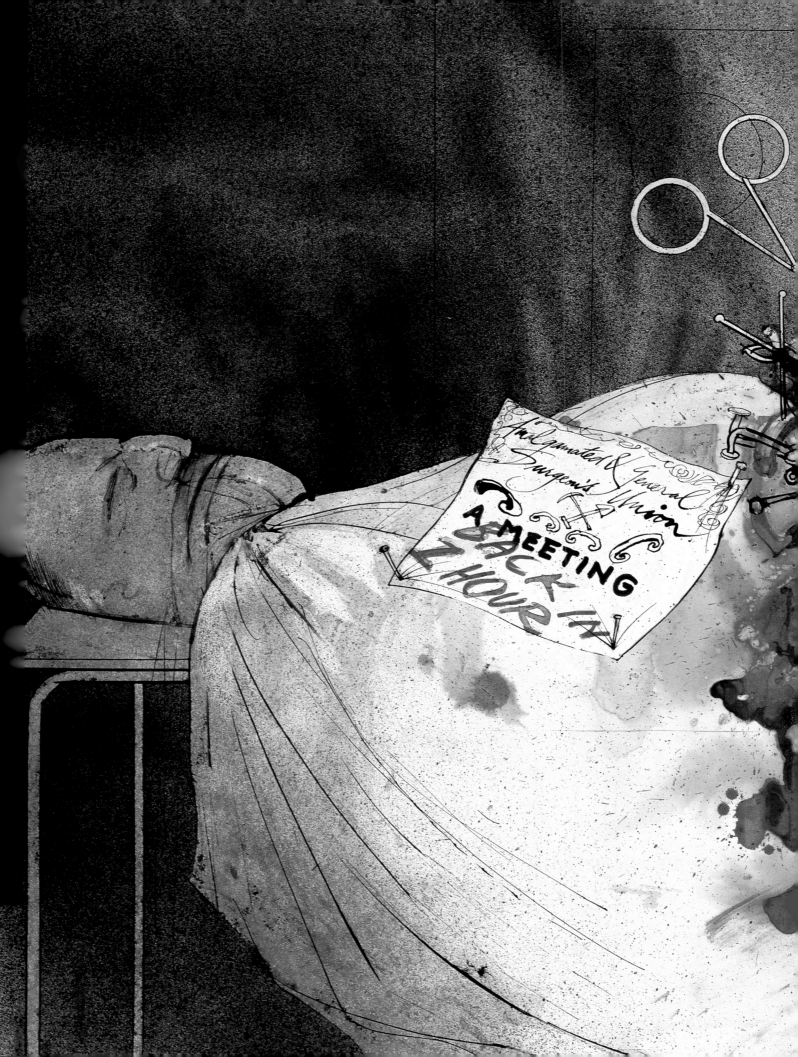

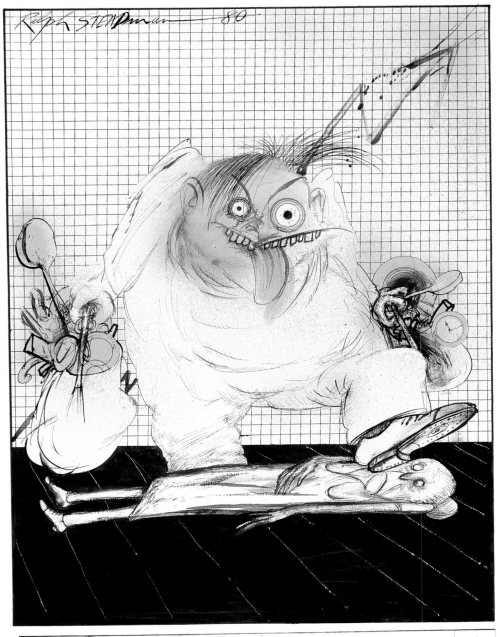

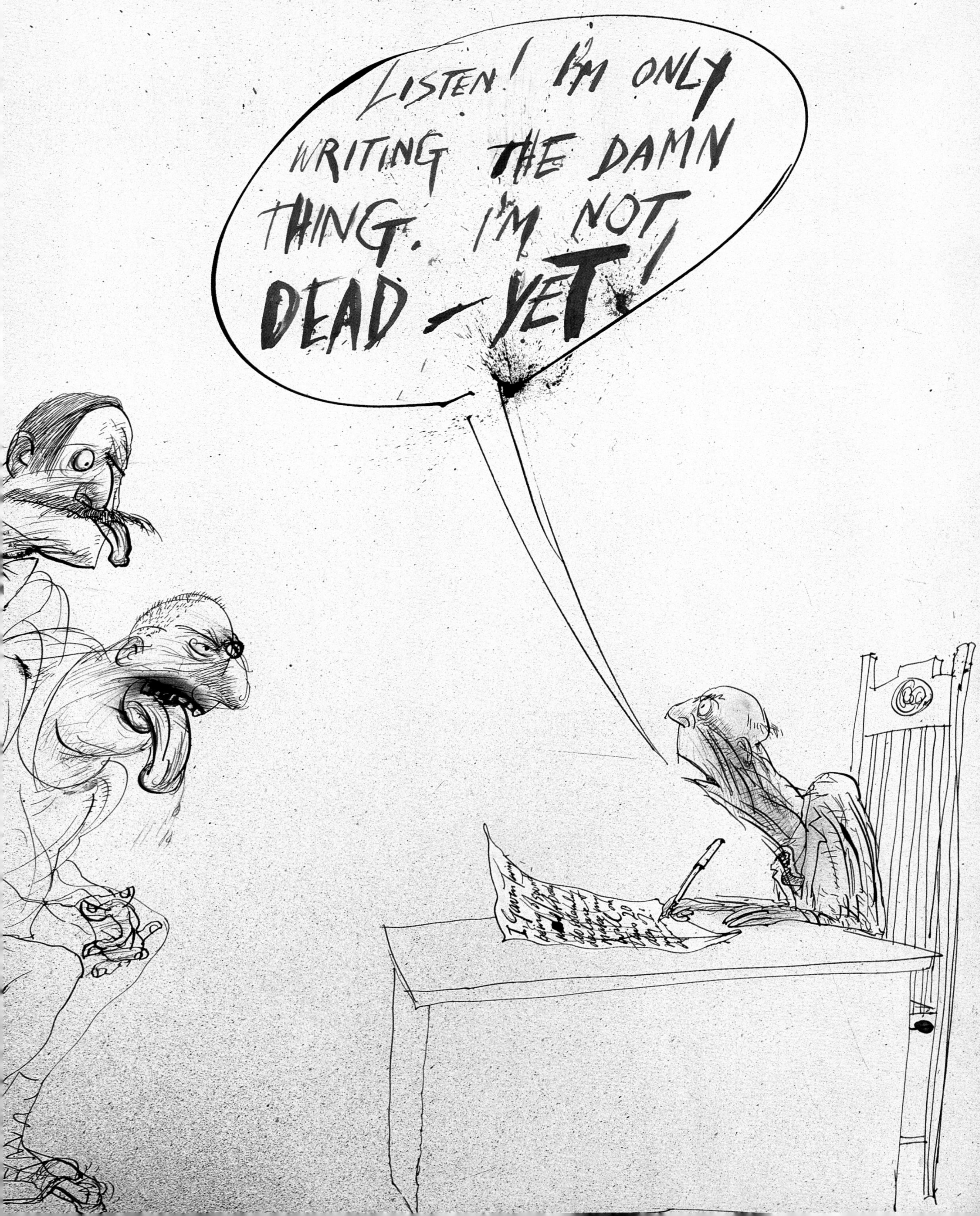
LISTEN! I'M ONLY WRITING THE DAMN THING. I'M NOT DEAD – YET!

GOOD EVENING -ER- THE FUCK-UP STARTS HERE- -ER-